Celebrate
2000

Two Thousand Things to Think About, Learn and Do for the Year 2000

Written by Robynne Eagan

Illustrated by Mike Artell

Teaching & Learning Company

1204 Buchanan St., P.O. Box 10
Carthage, IL 62321-0010

This book belongs to

_____

Foreword

It's the book you have been waiting 2000 years for! *Celebrate 2000* is for people everywhere who want to run with the exciting year 2000 theme. The book will take you on a journey through enlightening information and exciting activities to help you learn about and celebrate the year 2000. This book will guide children and educators through the past and present and prepare them to blast into the future.

Acknowledgements

I would like to thank all of those who went before and those who, as I write, continue to raise awareness of the issues that are most important for humanity and our planet. I would like to thank those who have left a trail for us to follow through the last 2000 years so that we may know about life before and make life yet to come a little better. I would like to acknowledge the assistance of Teresa Healy, Professor of Political Studies at Trent University, Peterborough, Canada, for asking stimulating questions and sharing her knowledge. A special thanks to Teresa, for leading many people to question where they need to question and to find the seeds of hope that are always present. A final thank you is extended to Tracey Schofield for her professional guidance and her kindness in sharing her creative activities with children of the new millennium.

Cover designed by Teresa Brierton

Copyright © 1998, Teaching & Learning Company

ISBN No. 1-57310-109-5

Printing No. 98765432

Teaching & Learning Company
1204 Buchanan St., P.O. Box 10
Carthage, IL 62321-0010

Table of Contents

Dear Teacher or Parent,

The year 2000 is almost here! Teaching and learning on the verge of a new millennium is the event of a lifetime. This infamous, long awaited year has long represented "the future." For centuries just the mention of it has stimulated imaginations and with its arrival the world as we know it may never be the same! The year 2000 opens a door to the future and inspires us to look at who we were, who we are and who we hope to be.

Celebrate 2000 is prepared to help educators run with the exciting year 2000 theme. The book looks at the human journey through history and into the future. This theme poses many interesting learning opportunities to help children better understand the world they live in. This book will inspire children to think, wonder and look at our history and future from an exciting vantage point in time.

The book is set up to provide information followed by educational enhancement activities:

Discussions ask questions crafted to stimulate young minds to creatively explore the past, the present and the future. Explore these questions before providing answers.

Activities provide enlightening extension projects designed to enhance the understanding of concepts and allow for development of hands-on skills.

Challenge questions will stimulate thought and develop independent problem-solving skills.

Research Topics are offered as strands of the main concept that could be further studied through development activities.

Try This provides suggestions for follow-up, enhancement or just-for-fun related activities.

The generation of children who venture into the year 2000 will do so with the problems, tragedies and triumphs of 20th century society at their heels. May this book help these children to manage the limitations and possibilities of this world and venture into the new millennium with the enthusiasm, knowledge, creativity and joy needed to make the dawning millennium a wonderful chapter in the book of human history.

Join the celebration and catch the wave of excitement to make the most of the year 2000!

Happy New Year!

Robynne

Robynne Eagan

Chapter 1: The Year 2000, What Does It All Mean?

The Year 2000!

You probably hear that phrase just about everywhere these days! Have you ever wondered what the year 2000 really is and why everyone is getting so excited?

The year that follows 1999 isn't just any year–it's a year that represents the end of an old era and the beginning of a new one. We are on the verge of a new millennium, and people just can't contain their excitement! Kids using this book have probably lived for about a decade or so (that's 10 years) but since long before they were born people have been thinking and talking about flipping their calendars to the year 2000.

According to the common calendar, a new millennium has dawned only once before–about 1000 years ago, when the calendar turned to the year 1000 A.D. There was a lot of excitement, but historians can't agree on whether people welcomed the new year with celebration or feared it as they did many unknown phenomena at that time. The end of the Dark Ages and the dawn of the Middle Ages may have been brought on by the new millennium.

Most people will be celebrating the year 2000 as the year of the new millennium even though the new millennium, technically speaking, won't arrive until January 1, 2001. Almost everyone is aware of this little fact but will be celebrating anyway. Year 2000 has a nice ring to it and for us 10-fingered followers of the decimal number system, the number 10 rules. Years that end with 0 carry particular significance. The year 2000, with all of those zeros, holds a special charm for us even if it doesn't really launch the beginning of a new decade, century *or* millennium.

The year 2000 launches us into our 2000th year of time. You won't see big changes overnight, but there will be a sense of something new–after all, 1000 years in the human story is nothing to take lightly. The last millennium brought many changes that could not even have been imagined in the year 1001–who knows what this millennium will bring!

The Beginning of Time

The phrase *the beginning of time* implies that there was an actual beginning to the elusive quality we call time. That's a difficult concept for anyone to get their mind around–even the famous thinker Albert Einstein! There are, in fact, several *perceived* beginnings to time.

Discussion

When do you think time began?

The Beginning of the Universe

Astronomers think about the beginning of time as the origin of our universe and have developed several theories to explain this beginning; the Big Bang Theory, the Oscillating Universe Theory and the Steady State Theory being among the most popular. Scientific evidence indicates that there was a definite beginning to the universe–believed to be about 15 billion years ago–and it has been expanding and getting older ever since.

The Beginning of Earth

Some people consider the formation of the planet we live on to be the beginning of time. By calculating the age of rock found on Earth, experts have determined that the Earth was formed from a huge cloud of dust and gas floating in space about four and a half billion years ago.

The Beginning of Humanity

Throughout history, people have believed that the Earth and life on it were created by gods. Today many people believe in Charles Darwin's theory of evolution which suggests that the human species evolved over billions of years from single-cell organisms in the oceans. Scientists have unearthed evidence to indicate that ape-like humans roamed in Africa about five million years ago. It is believed that these human-like apes evolved into the Homo sapiens of 40,000 years ago who are thought to be the ancestors of today's modern humans. Many who believe in Darwinism also believe that humans have a divine connection that gives us a special awareness of ourselves and differentiates us from the rest of the animal kingdom.

The Beginning of Calendar Time

Some people like to think about time in terms of recorded time. Early civilizations often began measuring time from the date of a very important happening in their culture. According to our current calendar system of marking the years, the Gregorian calendar, time began in the year 1–with the birth of Christ.

The End of Time

If time has a beginning, does it have an end? Time seems to have a definite beginning and ending for human life but maybe not for the universe. The universe has been expanding ever since it began 15 billion years ago and time has been moving forward ever since. Some scientists speculate that if the universe collapsed it would start to expand again like a giant spring. What do you think?

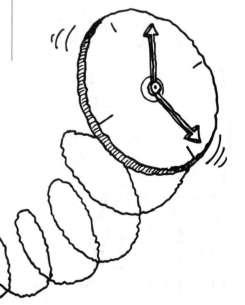

6

2000 Years and Counting

Now that you are all excited about the passage of time that has led us to the year 2000, you might just find yourself wondering when we started counting these years. It's a very good question. You probably know that time began long before 2000 years ago–so what does the year 2000 mean exactly? Two thousand years since what or when?

To better understand the counting of these years, we look to the calendar. About 5000 years ago humans started to measure time from one day to the next, from one "moon" to the next, one season to the next, one year to the next. The timekeepers used to help calculate and keep track of these time measurements were called calendars. Calendars helped people know when to plant and harvest their crops, when to expect particular weather and animal migrations and when to celebrate.

A year is the reliable unit of time that it takes Earth to travel once around the sun–365.26 days. It was the Romans who decided to give numbers to the passing years to help them keep track of time and events. In most civilizations people began measuring time from an important event, such as the birth or death of a hero or leader or the founding of a city.

The Romans numbered the years from the time of the founding of the Roman Empire and counted for 1288 years. By 1200 the Roman Empire had become a Christian Empire and a monk by the name of Dionysius Exiguus suggested that the year should be numbered from the year of the birth of Jesus Christ, worshiped by the Christians. Based on what little information was available, Dionysius settled on 754 as the probable year of Christ's birth and this date marked the beginning of our calendar time. This marked 754 as the year 1 A.D. and turned the year 1288 based on the founding of the city to 534 A.D. Our time began with the event of the birth of Christ in the year 1 A.D. Events that happened before year 1 are referred to as *B.C.* meaning "before Christ" and dates following year 1 are referred to as *A.D.* for "anno domini," the latin term meaning "the year of our Lord." Today some people use *B.C.E.* or *C.E.* meaning "Before the Common Era" and "the Common Era."

This calendar numbering system, modified by Pope Gregory, has been in usage since 534 A.D. This Gregorian calendar is now considered the common world calendar which means that most of us will be celebrating the year 2000 at the same time!

Even though modern scholars believe that Christ's birth may be 4 to 20 years off of the year 1 A.D., that year is accepted as the symbolic birthday of Christ and for Christians, the year 2000 will also mark the 2000th birthday of Christ–that's a lot of candles!

Although the common calendar has become a standard, other local and religious calendars are still in use. When the common calendar reaches the year 2000, the Muslim calendar will read 1421, the Hebrew calendar 5760, the Hindu calendar 1921 and the Chinese calendar 4698. What year is it for you?

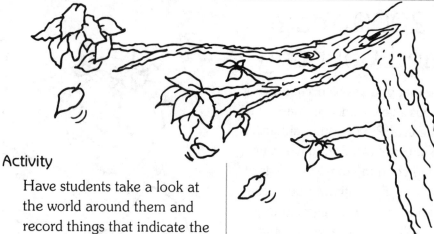

Counting the Days?

Humans were aware of the passing of hours in a day long before clocks were invented, and they were aware of the passing of days long before calendars came to be.

Discussion

If there were no clocks today, what things would let you know that the day was passing by? Discuss the signs around you that mark the passing of the days. How about daylight and darkness, sunrise and sunset, changes in plants and animal and human behavior?

It is pretty easy to notice the coming and going of each day even if you don't have access to a watch, but what about the passing of the days? If you didn't have a calendar, how would you notice how many days have passed? What signs would indicate that many days had passed?

With the passage of time, things and people begin to get older—or age. Things that are young or new change and become old as time passes. Some things change a lot and some change very little.

Observing changes in the things around you is one way of noticing the passage of time.

Activity

Have students take a look at the world around them and record things that indicate the passing of the hours and days.

Have students record signs that indicate the passage of time. Present opportunities for children to consider the growth of plants and human beings (including themselves) and the passing of the seasons.

HEY... THE LEAVES ARE FALLING AGAIN...

Mark the Passing Days

Now that you are noticing the passage of the minutes, hours and days, how are you going to mark this passage?

Discussion

If you were unable to use the calendar, how might you mark the passing of the days?

Activity

Keep track of the passing days using a tally, bottle tops dropped into a bottle, pennies taped to a board or another method that arises from the discussion above.

Research

Long before humans had calendars on the wall or watches on their wrists, they were keeping track of time. Find out how early people tracked and marked time.

In c. A.D. 100 the sandglass timer was developed in Rome and timekeeping as we know it was on its way.

1000-Day Countdown

On April 6, 1997, a long countdown began in many places around the world–the 1000-day countdown to the year 2000. Those 1000 days have been given special significance as a time to prepare for the new millennium. Countries, organizations and citizens are taking these days to think and act for peace, community service, spiritual rejuvenation, kindness, the environment and other important aspects of life on this planet. A giant digital clock 109 feet long and 40 feet high has been erected on the Eiffel Tower in Paris to tick away the 1000 days. And beneath the waters of the river Liffey in Dublin, Ireland, another digital giant is tick-tocking towards the year 2000 ready to send off a fireworks display on the stroke of midnight December 31, 1999.

Activity

President Clinton of the United States has urged American citizens to use this countdown to a new millennium to build a better future for us all. Make a list of 1000 things you can do to build that better future.

In ancient Egypt the lotus flower shape represented the number 1000.

*The word **millennium** comes from the Latin word **mile** meaning "one thousand." Can you find any other words that have come from the root word?*

*The words **milestone** and **milepost** derive from the ancient Roman practice of placing a marker every thousandth stone, so the year 2000 is a milestone year!*

Activity

In the spirit of the 1000-day countdown, compose a list of 1000 things to do to prepare for the new millennium. Provide one thing to do for each day remaining until the year 2000.

Provide each child with a copy of this group project so they can carry on their preparations after your school year ends.

The Greek word *chronos* has come to mean "time" and is used in many time-related words. Can you think of any such words?

Name _____

The Month of _____, _____

Fill in the name of the month and year and mark the passing days on the grid using a system of your choice. Include details on your calendar that are important to your life.

Saturday					
Friday					
Thursday					
Wednesday					
Tuesday					
Monday					
Sunday					

10

Counting the Centuries

A century is a time period of 100 years that begins with the year unit of 1. Years 1 to 100 are referred to as the 1st century, the years 101 to 200 as the 2nd and so on, the years 1901 to 2000 as the 20th and so on.

Challenge

Using the pattern above, find out what century you are living in now. You will discover that you are living in the 20th century. In what centuries did the years 642 A.D. and 1222 fall? On what date does this century end? When does the 21st century begin?

Research

How many years are in a decade, century and millennium? Can you find any other time terms that indicate a particular number of years?

The Clock of Centuries

Materials

library or research materials

large round disk, such as cardboard from a pizza

protractor

glue

scissors

Get Started

Use a protractor to divide the disc into 10 equal sections.

Label the first section 11th century, the second 12th century and so on to the 20th century.

Divide the participants into groups of no more than four children.

What to Do

1. Assign each group a particular century to research.

2. Have each group record their findings on the appropriate space on the millennium wheel. They can draw pictures or write key words to capture information about the particular era in history.

3. Have the groups report their findings to the class in chronological order.

Try This

- Display the wheels for all to see.

- Choose to research the first millennium in the same manner.

The Millennium Mix-Up

We're all a little early–a year early in fact with our millennium celebration! January 1, 2000, is not the beginning of a new decade, century or millennium–it's just another year–our 2000th year! Our calendar has a little problem that has a lot of people confused when it comes to counting the decades, centuries and millenniums.

In the 1900s we are living in what is called the 20th century. We are at the end of that century and looking forward to entering the new century. Not only are we about to enter the new century–we are also about to enter a new millennium–so getting the right date is more important than ever!

People will be celebrating the year 2000 with great excitement and enthusiasm, but the truth of the matter is that we will not really be entering the new millennium until January 1 in the year 2001! Only on that date can we say that time, according to our calendar, began 2000 years ago.

Our calendar began with the year 1 A.D., not the year 0. This means that when the year 2 began–only one year had passed from the beginning of our "calendar time." By the year 2000 only 1999 years will have passed since our year counting began. Without that year 0, our centuries and millennia don't really change until the 01 years instead of the 00

years. This makes the year 2000 the last of the old millennium, not the first of the new millennium.

A little confused? Think of the calendar as a baby that came into the world already being one year old! We begin our life at the age of 0 and start counting from there. When we turn one-year-old, we have been living for one year and will be entering our second year of life. The calendar began as a "one-year-old" and was really only one year old when it turned two years of age! You can subtract one year from the calendar year to find out how many years have passed in our calendar.

You can clear up the understanding of this mix-up by taking a look at these time lines:

Most people will celebrate the year 2000 even though "our time" will only be 1999 years old on that date. The excitement of all of those nines turning to zeros is more than most of us can bear–so we're going to celebrate anyway!

Challenge

How old would you be now if you started life as a one-year-old? How many years would you have lived by now? Your age and the time you lived won't match!

THE IMPORTANT QUESTION IS...WHERE ARE ALL THE BIRTHDAY PRESENTS?

Calendar

The calendar is 2.

1_____2_____3

    1 year

You

You are 1.

0_____1_____2

    1 year

TLC10109 Copyright © Teaching & Learning Company, Carthage, IL 62321-0010

Who's Counting?

The year 2000 wouldn't mean a thing to us if we didn't have a counting system. Whether you have noticed it or not, you're surrounded by numbers and counting!

Discussion

Think about the numbers and counting that fill your life; the clock counts the minutes from the time you awake until you go to bed, the calendar counts the days, the speedometer indicates your speed, numbered radio frequencies denote the airwave bands, the thermometer reveals the temperature, money indicates value, birth dates indicate your age . . . the list seems endless.

Challenge

Imagine your world without a counting system. What would it be like?

Activity

Try to get through a day without using numbers or counting.

For thousands of years early civilizations existed without a system to record numbers. People were more flexible and did not need to know or record precise numbers. These early people developed methods of accuracy as needed based on their intuition and experience. In time, as life became more complicated, methods were devised to estimate, compare and record information needed to count livestock, produce, days and wealth. Notches marked on wood, bone, clay or rock helped people to keep track of quantities. This tally keeping led to the written number system first used about 5000 years ago.

Roman Numerals

Roman numerals were devised by the Romans over 2000 years ago and are still found in usage today. This system was based on seven symbols, consisting of straight lines that were easy to mark into stone or wax.

I = 1	L = 50	M = 1000
V = 5	C = 100	
X = 10	D = 500	

The seven numerals are combined in various ways to show larger or smaller numbers. When the numeral on the right is of equal or less value to the numeral on the left, then the numerals are added. If the numeral on the left is of less value than that on the right, it is subtracted from the larger value, i.e. IV = 4 and XI = 11.

Activity

Where are Roman numerals used today? Search for these numerals in your life.

Challenge

Find the values for these Roman numerals: XV, IX, MCMXCIX, MM. In the western world, Roman numerals were replaced by the Arabic numerals you are familiar with.

Arabic numerals were developed by Indian and Hindu mathematicians in about 500 A.D. and brought to Europe by Arabs in about 1200 A.D.

Let's Take a Look at 2000

How much is 2000? How old is 2000? How big is 2000? It's a pretty big number to picture in your head!

Let's Count   Look at your fingers–there should be 10 of them. Count to 100 hundred by 10s. Can you picture that many fingers in your head? OK, now count to 2000 by 100s. Can you picture *that* many fingers in your head?

Imagine That?   I think that there are 2000 people in a _____.

I think that there are 2000 leaves on a _____.

I could probably fit 2000 jelly beans in a _____.

2000 pennies stacked up would be about as tall as _____.

Measure It!   2000 steps will take me _____.

_____ is about 2000 centimeters high.

_____ is about 2000 feet long.

_____ is about 2000 miles away.

Weigh It!   _____ weighs

about 2000 _____.

Spend It!   2000 dollars will buy _____.

Picture It!   2000 pennies would stack up to be as high as _____.

Wish for It!   I wish I had 2000 _____.

Name _____

Let's Explore 2000!
Help Wanted!
Counters needed to answer
questions about 2000.

2000 and Counting . . .

How long does it take you to count from 100 to 110? _____

How long does it take you to count from 1900 to 1910? _____

There are _____ seconds in one minute.

There are _____ minutes in one hour.

There are _____ hours in one day.

About how long would it take you to count from 1 to 2000? _____

2000 Years Is a Long Time!

Can you imagine 2000 years? Think about it in terms of the days, hours, minutes and seconds that we know so well.

Estimate and then calculate the following:

Write your estimate on the first line and your calculation on the second line.

A year is _____ _____ days.

A day is _____ _____ hours or _____ _____ minutes or _____ _____ seconds.

2000 years is _____ _____ days.

2000 days will equal _____ _____ years and _____ _____ days.

If Only I Had 2000 Years

2000 years is long enough for _____ generations to live upon the Earth, long enough for

_____ and long enough for _____.

Exploring 2000

Calendar Boogie

Look to your calendar to help you understand the passing of the years. Each block represents a day, each page represents a month and the entire calendar represents a year. How many times would you have to flip through all of the months to mark the passing of 2000 years?

Search for 2000

Have children think about, explore and answer the following statement:

There are 2000 . . .

If I Had 2000 . . .

Have children think about, discuss and/or write the statements for the following imagination stimulators . . .

If I had 2000 years to live, I would . . .

If I had 2000 cousins, I would . . .

If I had 2000 dollars, I would . . .

If I had 2000 acres, I would . . .

Collection Connection

A connection of collections can help your group visualize the number of the hour–2000!

You can gather 2000 items in your room with little effort and much excitement and interest. Your group of children may have had some experience with the 100th day of school in their earlier grades. How about a 2000 day?

Have 20 children each bring in a collection of 100 things. It would be best if the 100 items could be arranged in rows of 10.

How many items will you have if 20 children bring in 100 each?

2000 Wishes

Turn your classroom into a galaxy of wishes for the new millennium. Make star templates about 9" x 9" (22 x 22 cm). Have students trace and cut out stars from sturdy white paper. How many stars will each child need to make so you will have 2000 stars? Children will write their wishes for the millennium on the stars. The stars can be coated with glitter and hung from the ceiling.

2000 Flavors

Turn a bulletin board into an ice cream store front and have children make up 2000 fabulous flavors!

Chapter 2: The Past Comes Before the Future

We wouldn't be where we are today without the past behind us!

Let's Travel to the Past

To put the future into perspective, it is helpful to look to the time that has passed—we call this time "the past." Each of us has lived in the past, is currently living in the present and will one day be in the future. Life is a one-way journey through time!

Our planet and civilization have traveled from the past, into the present and are heading for the future. The civilization that we live in today has a lot to do with everything that happened from the beginning of time, so let's take a peek into the past.

I'M EVOLVING... DO YOU THINK THE TIE HELPS?

Back Beyond 2000

The 2000 years that have been marked by our calendar are filled with a lot of history; but it's nothing compared to the years and events that stacked up before that! The last 2000 years was a very, very short time in the evolution of the Earth.

Way back, billions of years ago, our universe had its beginnings and about five billion years ago the formation of Earth took place. Over that five billion years there have been many changes on this planet we call home. Our planet is always evolving and changing. On the Earth's surface continents are drifting at a pace so slow and over an amount of time so long that we cannot detect it and can barely imagine it. On these continents and in the waters life-forms evolve from previous ones and species inherit traits—at a pace so slow that these changes are not detectable in lifetime.

Human Life on Earth

Scientists have long debated the age of the human race. In 1859 Charles Darwin introduced the idea of evolution with his publication *Origin of the Species*. His theory explains that humans evolved over billions of years from the oceans to land dwellers.

The first human-like beings, named *Hominidae*, are believed to have evolved about six million years ago, followed by Australopithecus of Africa who left the first footprint in history about three million B.C. Homo habilis of about two million years ago was the first to use tools and had a brain about half the size of the modern brain. About 1.5 million years ago, Homo erectus, an upright ancestor, more closely related to the modern human, lived in China, Japan, Africa, Europe and southeast Asia. This being is believed to be the first to harness fire. More recently, beginning about 150,000 years ago, Neanderthals of Europe evolved—looking much like the modern human, wearing clothing, caring for their sick and marking the graves of their dead. The tall and erect Homo sapiens or "wise humans" evolved from 40,000 to 100,000 years ago. They communicated through speech and art and are believed to have shared a system of beliefs. It is widely believed that the many peoples of the Earth originated from this common ancestor.

*The term **history** refers to the time in human development after the invention of writing. It comes from the Greek word **histo** meaning "know this" or "I have seen."*

The History of Humanity

The world's past is separated into *history* and *prehistory*. *Prehistory* refers to the time before humans left a written record of their lives and times. This time period covers the first 35,000 years of human existence. Archaeologists piece together the story of these early times by making educated guesses based on evidence that they unearth.

Some events in the course of human history changed the world in important ways–the invention of writing was one such event. Modern humans appeared about 40,000 years ago but written history emerged only about 5000 years ago or thereabouts in different places. Writing provided early people with a means to record details pertaining to commerce, laws, dates and important events.

Prehistoric Human Times

By 33,000 B.C. Homo sapiens were living a nomadic life-style in search of food that led them to inhabit most of the globe. Between about 40,000 to 2000 B.C., these hunters traveled from Siberia across the Bering strait into the Americas.

The Prehistoric Ancient World dawned as the Ice Age waned and early humans mastered fire for warmth, cooking and protection and discovered that survival was easier when they banded together. In the Southern Hemisphere between 10 and 8000 B.C., lands along river systems became fertile grounds for human development. Farming gradually replaced hunting as a way of life allowing for settlement in shelters and villages.

Discussion

What do you think the term *The Cradle of Civilization* means?

How does the perspective of the writer affect written history?

Early Civilization; 5000 B.C. to 50 B.C.

One of the most important turning points in human history occurred when early people settled into organized villages where people had specific tasks and social responsibilities. These organized settlements sprang up at different times about 5000 B.C. throughout the world and became our first civilizations. These settlements gave rise to two of the greatest inventions in human development, the inventions of writing and the wheel. By about 1000 B.C. most early humans were raising crops and animals. Trade and immigration brought growth and diversification and with these advancements came conflicts, power struggles and the harnessing of the natural environment.

3500 B.C.	The invention of the first wheeled vehicles
3500 B.C.	Writing developed in Sumer, China; (c. 3250 B.C.); Egypt (2000 B.C.); Crete (1300 B.C.); Mexico (c. 1150 B.C.)
c. 3000 B.C.	Rise of civilizations of early Sumer and Kingdoms of Egypt
c. 2500 B.C.	Great civilizations and empires began to emerge in Africa
c. 2000 B.C.	Villages, empires and civilizations of the Americas emerged, most notably that of the Mayan culture in Central America

NICE IDEA, BUT IT NEEDS SOME WORK.

2000 Years of Civilization

Many changes occurred between the evolution of the human and the development of civilizations. The kind of societies we live in today throughout the various continents arose from the ebb and flow of civilizations that came before us. North American society has been particularly influenced by the early immigrants and the ideals of the Greek and Roman societies which gave rise to the Medieval society of western Europe. It is impossible in the space of this chapter to do justice to all the influences that have given life to our society. Allow your group to shape its own discussions, form its own questions and look at their individual histories in the course of your society.

The First Millennium; Years 1 to 1000

Discussion

If you could travel back to the year 1 A.D., what might you expect to see?

The Dark Ages; A.D. 476 to 1000 A.D.

The Dark Ages, or Early Middle Ages, followed the fall of the Roman Empire. Few historical records were kept or survived the era that witnessed the end of the ancient world and the rise of the modern world. The 5th century saw Europe in the throes of wars, conflicts and battles in which "barbarians" sought to establish kingdoms based on Roman laws and customs. Many of the "barbarian" invaders were skilled farmers and crafts people who gave rise to the Byzantine Empire.

While Europe lived through the conflicts of the Dark Ages, Chinese and Arab civilizations made discoveries in science, technology, medicine and astronomy that would, in time, be passed on to Europe. Although the European Dark Ages were a time of few advancements it was here that modern Western civilization had its beginnings.

The Greeks were the first society to develop the democratic system of government that forms the foundation of modern Western civilization. Their ideas, institutions, values and beliefs had a great impact on those of the modern world.

Research Topics

Preservation of literature and texts by Irish monks during the Dark Ages
Alexander the Great
Democracy

Let's take a look at the first millennium!

5000 B.C.-A.D. 100	Ancient civilizations continued to flourish up until about A.D. 100
	The Classical World influence remained until about A.D. 500
58-50 B.C.	Roman Era begins. Julius Caesar conquers Gaul and lands in Britain.
c. A.D. 98-117	Under emperor Trajan, Roman Empire reached its greatest extent
A.D. 476	Rome fell to the Goths and the Dark Ages began in Europe
A.D. 476-1453	The Byzantine Empire is ruled in the traditions of the Roman Empire in the East

The Middle Ages; 1000 to 1460

Following the Dark Ages came the Middle Ages or Medieval Period. Medieval Europe is viewed as the birthplace of our modern civilization. By 1000 A.D. a new society had taken root in what was left of the civilizations of the ancient world.

The emergent society developed under the Greek ideals of freedom and beauty and the Roman principles of Christianity. The culture, ideas, laws, education systems and government that arose formed the basis for the modern European society we know today. Medieval villages were united under powerful lords. Empires rose and fell throughout the world and a sense of belonging to a wider community became important.

It was a time of travel, trade and exploration throughout the continents with scholars exploring ancient learning and crusaders traveling to enlightened centers of Islam. Modern agricultural practices took root. Wind, water and the horse were harnessed for power.

Activity

Host a Medieval Festival with your group. Wear the clothing (and armor) of the day, share foods and engage in Middle Ages activities such as trade, archery and crusades. What cause might be worth *crusading* for today?

Research Topics

King Charlemagne
Joan of Arc
Feudal System
Black Death
Mongol Empire
Gutenberg's printing press (1454)

A.D. 1066	Normans conquered England
A.D. 1215	The Magna Carta (Great Charter) signed in Britain
A.D. c. 1300	Creation of the Aztec Empire, Mexico and Inca Empire in Peru
A.D. 1381	Peasants' Revolt in England
A.D. 1300	Benin Kingdom founded in West Africa
A.D. 1368-1644	Ming emperors rule China

The past is but the beginning of a beginning,
and all that is and has been is but twilight of the dawn.

H.G. Wells, *The Discovery of the Future*, 1901

Modern History; 1453 to 1600

A new age dawned between the 14th and 16th centuries in a period referred to as the Renaissance. The rebirth of learning and culture began in Italy where scholars studied the classical writers, artists and philosophers of ancient Greece and Rome. These great thinkers experimented and made advancements in many areas of study, inspiring a rebirth of classical ideas and thought that spread throughout Europe. Along with new ideas and advancements, this era saw conquests and cruel abuses of power.

Education was no longer linked to and controlled by the church as it had been in medieval times. People began to challenge accepted beliefs, study and explore new worlds and revive culture and learning. Ideas became accessible to all who could read through the revolutionary invention of the printing press in 1454.

Beginning in the 1500s a new concept of political organization known as the city-state began to appear. Geographic regions were united and governed under a centralized governing power to which all citizens pledged allegiance—in Europe this power fell to the monarchy alone. From this came the concept of *nation* that began to spread throughout the world and by the 19th century had become the basis for most political organizations. A change from medieval to early modern times arose from the structure of the city-state and from the ideas of the Renaissance, the Reformation and the commercial revolution.

By 1500	Europe engaged in discoveries, modern industrialism, conquests, trade, colonization and exploitation that would affect much of the world.
1453	The Turks took Constantinople, ending the Byzantine Empire
1492	Christopher Columbus claimed the Caribbean for Spain and introduced European horses and weapons
1494	Treaty of Tordesillas divided the Americas between Spain and Portugal
1500s	The Voyages of Discovery brought Spanish and Portuguese settlers and soldiers to conquer many of the lands in Central America
1519	Ferdinand Magellan set sail on the first expedition around the world
1502-10	The first African slaves were taken to the Americas
1514	Nicolaus Copernicus's theory that the Earth orbits the sun was recorded in writing
1517	Martin Luther launched the Reformation in Germany

Research Topics

Aztec Empire of Mexico
Elizabethan Era
Explorer Amerigo Vespucci
Leonardo da Vinci
Reformation
Renaissance architecture

Conquest and Trade; A.D. 1600 to 1750s

European trade and conquest that had begun in the 1450s continued throughout this period in the Americas and on the African continent. Explorers traveled far and wide and empires rose and fell. The expansionism was followed by a period of struggles for a balance of power that lasted well into the 19th century.

The 17th and 18th centuries in Europe were known as the Baroque Period; a highly extravagant period in history recognized for its lavish style and complexities.

1600s	Slaves were taken from Africa to work in the Caribbean
1620	*Mayflower* ship arrived in New England, carrying the Puritan pilgrims from Britain
1648	The Treaty of Westphalia, considered the birth date of the nation-state
1649	Russians conquered Siberia and reached the Pacific Ocean
1642-1648	English Civil War
1687	Sir Isaac Newton's theory of gravity published

New Nations; 1750 to 1830s

Throughout the 18th and 19th centuries Europeans continued to trade, settle and rule many parts of the world but not without strife. By 1750 people began to react angrily to the European expansion, rebelling and fighting for their rights and freedoms. It was a time of revolutions, wars–and for many nations–the gaining of independence.

Outside the political arena, an agricultural revolution had changed the ways of farming in many parts of the world and a bond was forming between humans and machines that would have a great effect on most countries of the world.

Culturally, people returned to the balanced life-style of classical civilizations.

Revolutions are events or eras of great change or confrontation that bring great changes to a society's governing body, law of laws, social programs and system of beliefs. Revolutions and uprisings have shaped the nations in which we live today.

Research Topics

Benjamin Franklin
Harriet Tubman
Lewis and Clark

1750s	Industrial Revolution began in Britain
1775-1783	American War of Independence
1789-1799	French Revolution
1796	Napoleon Bonaparte begins conquests of Europe and the Mediterranean

The true test of civilization is . . . the kind of men (people) the country turns out.

Emerson, *Society and Solitude*, 1870

The 19th Century: Unification, Colonization and a Modern World

1830s	Native Americans evicted from homelands and forced onto reservations
1837-1901	Victorian Age
1861-1865	Civil War
1867	British North America Act
1899-1902	The Boer War

The Industrial Revolution began in Britain in the early 19th century and soon spread across Europe and to the United States bringing major social changes to most of the world. Through the agricultural and industrial revolutions, the work of peasants and crafts people was slowly being taken over by machines. Wind, water and steam power drove pumps in mines and workings in the textile factories. By 1870 it seemed that the Western world had entered a new era—an age of progress and prosperity based on the staggering advances in science and technology.

By 1820 the first swell of hopeful European immigrants landed on the shores of America—by 1930 32 million of them crossed the ocean. Many of these immigrants and American settlers traveled west to colonize, and a railroad soon spanned the continent threatening the traditional way of life of native inhabitants.

By 1870 Britain and France had created large empires around the world and were challenged by other European countries vying to establish colonial empires to supply the raw materials needed for factories. The African continent became desirable for colonization and raw materials, and by this time all but Ethiopia and Liberia had been divided amongst the European powers. Worldwide disputes erupted over territory controls and ownership and over the rights of the people within the nations.

During this time many colonies struggled with colonization or fought for independence and the trials and growth that accompanied self-government. The United States suffered through a Civil War between the North and the South. Canada, Australia, New Zealand and South Africa became dominions with the British Empire gaining control over their own affairs and the pieces of the world puzzle seemed to be falling into place.

Research Topics

Industrial Revolution
American Civil War
Native American beliefs about the land

The 20th Century

As the 20th century began people were optimistic about peace and were energized by the rise of modern industry. By 1914 World War I raged in Europe, followed by the Great Depression in the '30s and a second World War (1939-1945) that ended with the dropping of the atomic bomb on Hiroshima. The years after 1945 saw the rebuilding of the old world, political upheaval around the world and the Cold War between the East and the West. By 1945 the nation-states of Europe that had conquered and dominated most of the world were being challenged by the colonial empires that sought to free themselves and become independent nations.

The later 20th century has been marked by inventions, a division between the wealthier nations of the north and the poorer nations of the south, a shift of economic power toward Far East, changes in family structures and urgent environmental problems.

Progress in science and technology was amazing in this century that saw the first automobile on the road and a space station in space. Remarkable inventions have joined humans and machines as never before. It is unlikely that people living even 100 years ago could have imagined the world that we now take into a new millennium.

1900	Industrial Revolution continues, Victorian era ends
1912	Henry Ford produces the Model T Ford automobile
1914	World War I begins in Europe
1929	Wall Street stock market crashes
1939	Hitler invades Poland and World War II begins
1945	Atomic bomb dropped on Hiroshima in Japan ends the war
1947	India and Pakistan gain independence
1948	Jewish state of Israel founded
1949	Mao Tse-Tung creates People's Republic of China
1950	United States joins the Vietnam War
1969	Neil Armstrong becomes the first man to walk on the moon
1987	Intermediate-Range Nuclear Forces Treaty is signed with the Soviet Union
1989	Berlin Wall knocked down
1991	Apartheid abolished in South Africa

Discussion

Do you think the discoveries, innovations and problems of the last century will have much impact on the overall history of civilization?

How has life changed for the working class over the last century?

Research Topics

Wright brothers first flight in 1903
The effect of the automobile on society
Mohandas Gandhi and his campaign
    for Indian independence in 1921
United Nations
UNICEF

Museum 2000

Get Started

Take a trip into the past.

Prepare for this project by visiting a local museum. Look for and record the following items on your trip:

an exhibit from the earliest time represented in the museum
an object that is 2000 years old
an object that is 1000 years old
objects that helped to keep time
an exhibit focusing on the 18th century
an exhibit looking at the 19th century
an exhibit focusing on your century
an object that surprised you

Discussion

Memories allow us to recall the past. How can the past be shared with others?

How can we learn about our past? Is it important to know about our past? Why or why not?

How did you feel looking at objects from the past? Do you think it is worthwhile to preserve these objects? Why or why not?

One hundred years from now what objects from your childhood do you think might be on display in a museum?

Some museums focus on particular times or places; others cover a wide range of area and time.

How can we preserve the past?

Create Your Own Museum

Create Museum 2000 to represent a period of history from the last 2000 years of human history. Divide children into groups and assign each a particular topic or time frame and lead them to research materials.

Exhibits

Using their knowledge of a particular era, have tour guides prepare information and exhibits in pleasing creative displays.

Have your knowledgeable tour guides prepare to lead tours of their exhibits.

Props

Guides may provide brochures, maps, guide books, recordings and videos to enhance their exhibits.

Invitations

Invite other classes and parents to visit your museum. After a day in the life of a museum tour guide, children will have a thorough understanding of their material!

Out-of-Date

What is cool today may not be cool in the near future. When things have been a part of the past and are no longer "trendy," we say they are out-of-date.

Discussion

What things do you think will go out of style? What might last into the next generation?

Activity

Host an Out-of-Date Day where children wear clothing, shoes and other fashion accessories from the past.

Set up an Out-of-Date display. Children can contribute coins, stamps, magazines and other memorabilia. Share some out-of-date music and out-of-date treats. But be careful—some things came back in style after a time and your out-of-date party might start a trend all over again! This activity may facilitate communication between parents, grandparents and children as cool kids learn about the past.

Tales from the Past

Discussion

If inanimate objects could talk, what would you like to talk to? What natural object do you think could tell the most interesting tales from the past?

Which things do you think would possess the most wisdom?

Activity

Write a tale from the perspective of a rock in a riverbed, a tree in the forest, a rock cliff overlooking the ocean, a fossil on a shore or a field of green grass.

Long Ago

Discussion

Ask the simple question "What's Old?" You may be surprised to see how different individuals respond.

Activity

Encourage children to think about the past by copying and completing this sentence: "Long ago . . ."

Participants may discover that long ago to one person may not be long ago to someone else.

Can we step into the past? Well, sort of. We can look at photographs, videos and into our own memories–but we can't go back into the past–what has passed is in the past!

Chapter 3: The Here and Now!

There Is No Time Like the Present

We refer to the time that we are living in as "the present." The *present* is the elusive moment that we are living–right this second. At this time in history, life is changing more rapidly than it has at any other time in the history of the world. Our lives and environments are being altered by innovations and population growth as never before–so it is sometimes difficult to get a handle on the present!

Live for the Moment

Has anyone ever told you to live for the moment? Most kids are pretty good at it! Living for the moment means living in the present–not worrying about the future or the past. Living for the moment helps us to appreciate and savor every moment we are living.

A Moment in Time Bulletin Board

Capture the year on a bulletin board.

Get Started

Discuss the present era with your group. Talk about everyday life.

What things are different than they were when our parents were growing up?

What things have come back in style from another time?

What is cool right now? What is popular?

What is there hope for? What are we afraid of?

Is there anything going on in the world right now that may affect the future?

Have there been any recent discoveries?

Have any great voyages been undertaken?

What national and world events are worth noting?

What to Do

1. Cut out large numbers to represent the year that you are living in.

2. Have children contribute photographs, stories, poetry, art, news clippings, collages and other pertinent data to create a bulletin board that captures the year.

Secrets in Stone

Discussion

The present can be preserved in many ways. We can preserve the present in our minds as memories.

Some things can hold secrets, stories and information in this way. Talk about the ways that rocks, fossils, trees, trodden paths, footprints or tracks, photographs, buildings, records, diaries, ruins and old newspapers can capture the present.

I'M LIVING IN THE "PRESENT"... HA!

Lifetimes

The natural world is a continuous cycle of the new life, growth and decay that makes up the life span of all living things. A look at life spans can give children a perspective on passing through the present time frame to another.

Discussion

How do we measure the growth or aging of people?

We measure our age in intervals of one calendar year–365 days. That year between one birthday and the next may seem like a long time!

What is the usual life span of a human? Have children think about people in their lives. Who is young? Who is old? Who is the youngest and who is the oldest person they know?

Every living thing grows at its own speed and has its own average life span. Some things, like sunflowers and bean plants grow very quickly–in days, in fact and live short lives–usually the length of one growing season. Some things take a little longer to grow but still grow quite quickly, like baby ducklings that take eight weeks to become full grown and may live for several years.

Some things, like human beings, take years and years to grow. The average life span of a female is 79 years and the average of a male is 72 years.

Place in Time Line-Up Activity

Make a human time line to represent the ages of participants. The children become the time line that tells a time story about their beginnings in the world.

Materials

group of six or more

How To

1. Have students form a line that starts with the youngest child and ends with the eldest. Chances are most of the children in your group were born in the same year, so have them line up according to birth month and day if necessary.

2. Explain that the children who were born first have lived longer and are older than children who were born later.

Try This

- Have children move to the music and then regroup in this line as quickly as possible.

You can't know the future before you get there and then it becomes the present and in no time at all it is in your past!

Make a Time Line

Chronology is the arrangement of events in the order in which they occur in time. Time lines provide a linear chronological picture of the passage of time. These visual aids can provide a clear perspective of what went before, what is now and what might yet come.

Get Started

1. Look at some time lines for the history of the Earth or civilization.
2. Prepare the strips and materials.

Materials

narrow strips of paper about 2" (5 cm) wide

glue

writing and coloring instruments and stickers

measuring tool

What to Do

1. Glue strips together end to end to make your time line as long as you desire.
2. Have children decide what their time line will represent: their life, the school year, their family history, friendships, etc.
3. Turn your strips into time lines by marking equal time intervals along the strip; i.e. 1 inch = 1 year.
4. Label each mark with a number. The beginning of the strip should be labeled *0* and then numbered accordingly as you go in years, months, days, etc.
5. Complete the time line by recording important events at the appropriate time intervals. You can record events with drawings, photographs or text.

Try This

- Create time lines for your school year, the century, the millennium or the entire history of civilization!
- Make a *My Life Time Line,* marking one-year intervals. Mark the strip one year beyond the age of the child. Laminate it for a lasting momento of childhood.
- Fold a strip of paper into four quarters. Draw a sequential diagram showing how something has changed over time.

The Circle of Time

Many ancient societies did not think of time in a linear manner at all. They thought about time passage as a cyclical event. The passage of time was represented in many societies by circles or wheels of unending life.

Activity

Take a look at a native medicine wheel which shows the circular passage of time in terms of the cycles of the seasons and of life.

Find a tree trunk or bring a slice of trunk into your classroom and count the rings!

Each year that a tree lives it develops a layer or ring.

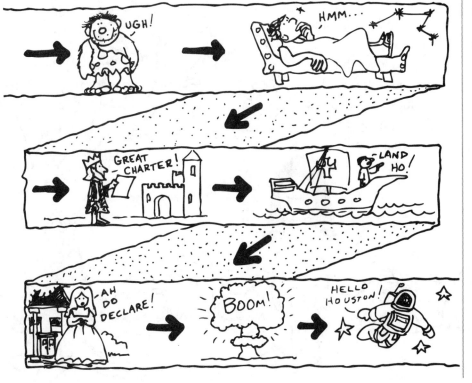

My Place on the Tree of Life

Children will enjoy learning about their ancestors as they explore the past and find their place in time.

Get Started

1. Ask children to think about their family or guardians–the people in the present to whom they are connected.

2. Now ask children to travel with you back to the past and think about their family. Who was their mother/father/guardian's mother or father? Did they have brothers or sisters? And who were their grandparents' parents? You won't want to go any further than this!

3. Send home the Family Tree Information Sheet on page 31. Allow two weeks for children and families to talk, dig out old photos and share family stories.

Materials

construction paper

markers

paste

scissors

photographs, photocopied photos or drawings of family members

Family Tree Information Sheets (page 31)

What to Do

1. Review the Family Tree Information Sheet with the children.

2. Explain that the tree is a way to put the child's family together so that it is easy to understand. Have students make their own unique family tree, transferring the information provided by their Family Tree Information Sheet to a "tree." Have children draw a tree trunk. They write their name on the trunk. The top of the trunk will contain names of siblings. The primary branches will contain the names of their parents and their siblings. Cousins can be included as apples hanging on the tree. If the child has information on two parents, the tree can be divided in half in some way: dark green/light green, high branches/drooping branches . . . Branches that rise above these will include the names of grandparents and great-grandparents.

Try This

- Children can decorate the tree and surrounding area to represent their family.
- Advanced students can include further details regarding grandparents and their siblings.

*A generation is the time frame of about 30 years–the time it takes for children to grow up and step into the shoes of their parents. The term **generation** also refers to a group of people in the same age group who share similar life experiences.*

YOU ARE HERE!

TREE OF LIFE

Name _____

Family Tree Information Sheet

Dear Parent/Guardian,

We are going into the past to learn more about our place in time. Please help your child to complete the following chart by _____. You may choose to explore one or two parents' or guardians' branches of the family tree for this project.

Please share a family story and, if possible, send a momento of your family sealed in a zip-type bag and labeled. Although we will take every precaution with these items, please do not send valued or irreplaceable treasures.

Thank you for your time and interest in this project; I hope you enjoy sharing your family history!

1. Child's name _____ Birth date _____

2. Siblings _____

_____

3. (Parent or Guardian) _____

4. _____'s siblings and children _____

_____

5. _____'s father _____

6. _____'s mother _____

Second "branch" of the family tree (optional)

7. (Parent or Guardian) _____

8. _____'s siblings and children _____

_____

9. _____'s father _____

10. _____'s mother _____

Capture Time in a Capsule

Who can pass up the opportunity to create a time capsule on the eve of a new era? A time capsule is a container that captures the essence of the here and now. Your capsule can capture events of the year, the century or the millennium for the future from a child's perspective. You may choose to capture life before the new millennium or on the first year of that millennium–either would be meaningful.

Get Started

Think about the time we are living in. What's it like being a kid today? How can we show people from another time (or planet) what life is like right now?

1. If you are putting together a group capsule, have each child contribute one item to represent their life right now.

   If individual capsules are being created, have children contribute a number of items for their own capsule.

   Remind children that items contributed to the time capsule will not be retuned. Do not accept any items which children or their families will want back if you truly plan to store the capsule into the distant future.

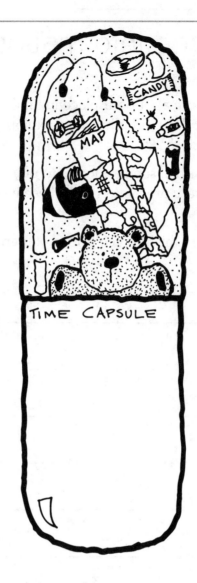

TIME CAPSULE

Consider the following items for your capsules:

- a postcard and/or map of your town

- photographs or hand-drawn pictures of you doing things you normally do

- a coin or commemorative stamp

- a magazine or newspaper article that describes life as it is for today's kids

- ticket stubs, toys, trinkets, candy wrappers or collector's items from the year

- a cassette recording, video or computer disc

- an item of clothing or footwear

2. Choose a safe place to store your capsule for discovery in the future: an attic, cellar, trunk, underground location or behind a stone or brick in a building.

What to Do

1. Have children gather materials using rubber bands, envelopes, paper clips or another organizational method. Label the items if necessary.

2. Have children complete the All About Me! form on page 33.

3. Gather the forms and materials in an envelope, box or jar.

4. Label the container with the date and year and decorate it.

5. Have a ceremonial dig or placement of the capsule in its resting place.

6. Sit back and wait for the future to unfold!

Try This

- Gather together in a year, two years, five years or in a decade to see how life has changed. Are you the same as you were when you captured time?

- Capture time with texture rubbings. Place a paper over bark, sidewalks, walls, inscriptions or coins and rub over the paper with a crayon to capture the texture.

All About Me!

My name is _____

I am _____ years of age.

I am living in the _____ century in the _____ millennium.

I live with _____

I am in grade _____ at _____

I spend most of my time _____

I like to _____

I don't like to _____

My favorite foods are: _____

My favorite drinks are: _____

I like to play _____

My favorite toys are: _____

My favorite hobbies are: _____

My favorite television shows are: _____

My favorite movies are: _____

My favorite books are: _____

I am afraid of _____

The worst problems facing the world today are: _____

_____

I would like to change the world by _____

_____

When I grow up, I would like to _____

_____

The best thing about being a kid today is _____

_____

Name _____

Time in a Bottle

What will you put in your time capsule?

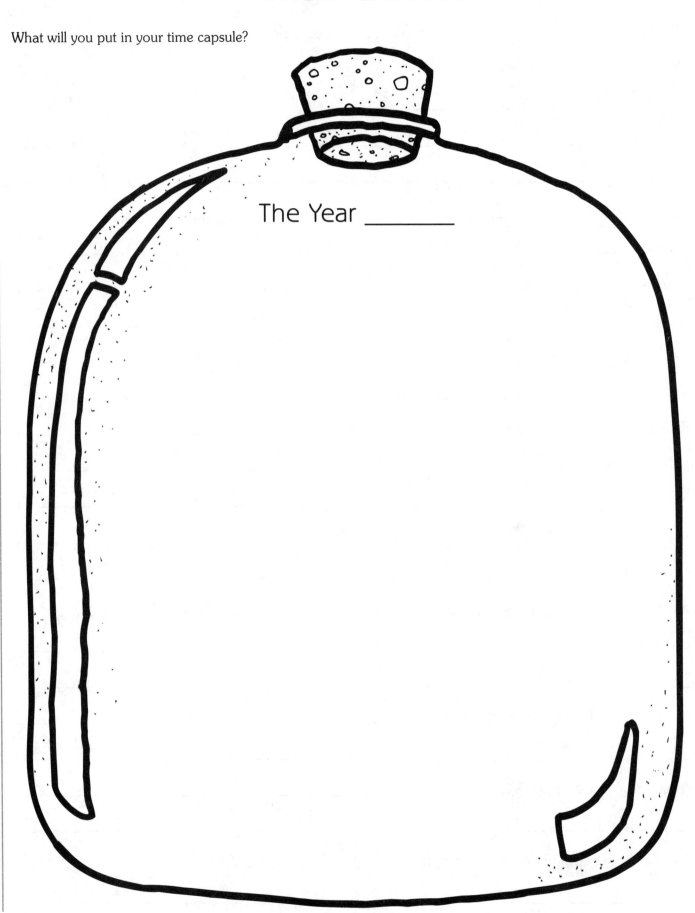

The Year _____

2000 Years of Invention, Innovation and Discovery

From the earliest civilization to the present day there have been a great many remarkable discoveries that have greatly altered the course of human history. Before the year 1, many important discoveries had already been made–the use of fire and tools, timekeepers and calendars and, of course, the wheel just to mention a few. But the last 2000 years have had their share of discoveries. Let's take a look at some important discoveries and inventions.

MAYBE I SHOULD HAVE INVENTED SOMETHING ELSE.

Many of the most important discoveries in civilization occurred before the year 1 A.D.

A.D. 100 The Mechanics of Machinery
Hero, the greatest inventor of the 1st century, discovered ways to convert energy into useful means with a lever, pulley, wedge, screw, windlass and steam turbine.

1760s Efficient Steam Engine
James Watt developed the first efficient steam engine to meet the power needs of the Industrial Revolution.

1796 Immunization
Edward Jenner's invention of the vaccine eventually leads to worldwide immunizations.

1876 Telephone
Alexander Graham Bell revolutionizes long distance communication.

1903 First Powered Airplane
The Wright brothers opened the airways for travel with their amazing first flight.

1908 The Model T Ford is mass produced in the United States.

1942 The atom is split making way for the atomic bomb and nuclear energy.

1946 ENIAC Launches the Computer Age
The first general-purpose electronic digital computer (Electronic Numerical Integrator and Calculator) was invented by Presper Edkert, Jr. and John Mauchly.

1969 Neil Armstrong becomes the first man to walk on the moon.

1971 The Microchip Changes Information Technology
Marcian Hoff in California revolutionized the computer industry with this invention.

1989 U.S. spaceprobe *Voyager II* passes the planet Neptune.

1983 The laptop computer finds its first laps in the United States.

1994 The Channel Tunnel opens travel between England and France.

1997 Scottish scientist clones sheep.

Invention 2000

Become a 21st century inventor!

Get Started

Discussion

Everything around us–from the shoes we wear to the satellites in space–was invented by someone like you or I who met a challenge, solved a problem or came up with a new idea.

What great inventions do you see a need for in the new millennium?

What great discoveries do you think await our civilization, and how will they change our lives?

Materials

- paper
- measuring and drawing instruments
- cutting tools (scissors, craft knife)
- collection of found materials: cardboard pieces and boxes, wood, buttons, cups, egg cartons, wire, string, cloth, balls, hinges, rubber, tack, dials
- fastening materials: string, glue, tacks, thread, paper fasteners, tape

What to Do

1. Think up your own invention!

   Observe your world carefully–is there a need you can cater to, a problem you can solve or an improvement you can make?

   Brainstorm and think creatively. How can you solve the problem or meet the need?

   Research and find the best reasonable solution.

2. **Design** your invention on paper. Draw a diagram and write a description.

3. **Make a model** of your invention and try it out.

Try This

- Have children share their inventions with one another.

Research Topics

Find out about one discovery that has had an enormous impact on the way we live our lives. When and where was it invented?

When do you think this was said, "Everything that can be invented has been invented"? Believe it or not this statement was made by the Commissioner of the U.S. Office of Patents in 1899! Do you think this commissioner was correct?

What's New? What's News?

Search through local newspapers, watch the news and talk to people. What's going on in the world today? What exciting new inventions, discoveries and happenings would be worth taking note of?

Activity

Have students divide into groups to cover sections of a *What's News?* newspaper of the year.

Check out the internet! Use your search engine to find information about just about anything you can think of. Check out the year 2000, Space Exploration or Inventions to keep up with any new developments.

What's Happening on Our Planet?

There's an explosion going on—a population explosion. There have long been concerns about the phenomenal growth rate of the world's population. A century ago there were 1.7 billion people in the world—now there are about 5.7 billion. That is a huge increase in a brief time span. The world's population continues to grow by about 100 million people each year.

All of these people will be requiring food and shelter. The United Nations estimates that by the year 2050 there might be 10 billion people on the planet—which would put greater demands on the amount of food, water, land and natural resources the Earth supplies. Some people are worried that the Earth won't be able to meet the demands of our increasing population.

Where will those necessities come from as the Earth's resources dwindle? Some experts believe that the Earth has more than enough resources to feed 11 billion people if they are managed properly.

Discussion

How will population increases affect communication? Transportation? The natural environment? Housing?

Research Topics

What is the population of your town? A major city near you? Tokyo? London? California? New York? Your country, state or province?

How do you expect these figures to change by the year 2000?

How's the Planet Holding Up?

Modern society praises technology and industry as wonders of civilization, but it is these very wonders combined with a population explosion that have allowed modern civilization to almost destroy the planet we call home. The 20th century has witnessed something never before seen in human history–large-scale deterioration and destruction of vital natural resources. It could be said that modern-day progress is not such a desirable thing after all.

In the latter half of the 20th century, people realized the Earth was in danger. At first people thought that scientists could solve the problems for us. Although scientists and others are searching for solutions, our environmental problems remain and in some cases have become more severe. Dedicated people around the world spend their lives trying to save the planet. Governments, environmental organizations and concerned citizens have established laws and programs to help the planet. Their efforts have made some progress in the struggle to keep our planet healthy. Unfortunately the environmental problems are progressing faster than we can manage.

People long assumed that by the year 2000 we would have discovered ways to eliminate air, water, land and noise pollution. Unfortunately, that has not yet happened. The chemical and industrial revolutions have proceeded faster than our society can cope with. Despite all of the modern-day progress, we are unable to cure the pollution of our air, land and water. Although we have made improvements in some areas, overall we are rapidly losing ground. We all need to get concerned before it's too late.

Discussion

How important do you think it is to protect our natural environment?

Do you think that our governments and citizens are taking our environmental problems as seriously as they should? Why or why not?

What can you do to help make the planet healthier in the new millennium?

How does "survival of the fittest" affect the world today?

What does it mean to "go green"?

Do you think we could leave this planet behind and head off to another in the future, if things get too bad here on Earth?

Research Topics

Natural resources
Waste management
Endangered species
Ozone depletion
Acid rain

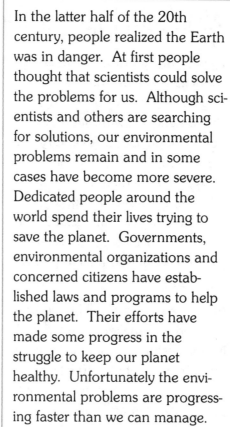

Chapter 4: Travel to the Future!

The past is behind us, the present is here; let's take a look beyond into the future.

The future is any time beyond the time we are currently experiencing–it can be seconds from now or it can be viewed in the context of a larger time frame implying any time yet to come–days, weeks, years, centuries or longer. As long as humans have lived they have wondered what the future had in store for them–in an hour, in a day or in the next harvest season.

The Future Is Here!

When people used to talk about the future–it was often represented by the symbolic year 2000. People expected many changes by that year; launched by innovations in technology, discoveries in science, advancements in education, changes in social structures, changes in governing policies and threats caused by pollution.

Discussion

Now that the futuristic date is upon us–how does it look?

Where do you think society is in its course of evolution?

Do you expect to see any major changes in our civilization in the near future?

Millennium Travelers

Materials

chalkboard display area and chalk

current and baby photographs of each participant

blutak™ or tape

Get Started

Have each child bring in a current and baby photo of themselves.

Use blutak™ to place the current pictures on one half of the chalkboard and the baby pictures on another. Use chalk to number each set of pictures.

Object

To match the corresponding numbers of baby pictures with the current pictures.

How to Play

1. Have participants draw chalk lines to connect the pictures they think match or record their matches on paper by using the numbers assigned to each picture.

2. The exercise can be "just for fun" or players can compete to see who matches the most pairs correctly.

Try This

• Connect the baby picture to the current likeness of each participant with yarn or string.

THE FUTURE

What Can We Expect in the New Millennium?

Throughout the history of civilization there have been advancements and catastrophes, celebrations and strife and alliances and conflicts which have contributed to the kind of society we live in today. As we enter the new millennium we should celebrate our achievements and address our 20th century problems.

The rise of modern industry changed the world in a way that few developments have in the course of human civilization. The commercial and industrial developments of the past 200 years have left the Earth with social, political, economic and environmental woes that we have only begun to wrestle with. The new millennium is called upon for laws and social controls for a new society, solutions to problems of overpopulation and an aging population, means to deal with racism, crime and violence and controls for highly destructive nuclear weaponry.

Discussion

What major events of this century have affected the way we live today?

How much has your society changed since the year 1900?

What changes have occurred in your lifetime?

Have machines helped or hurt humanity?

Do you think changing one event in time could have much impact on the future?

What can you do to make the future a better place?

Equality for All

Although many societies appear to offer equality for all, there are many factors that can stand in the way. Poverty is one such factor. The years since 1945 have been years of great prosperity for some but poverty for others—even in modern-day wealthy nations. Some believe that those stricken by poverty do not share in the dream of equality.

Gender or race may also stand in the way of equality. In the early 19th century only male property owners were allowed to vote. By the mid 19th century, a worldwide movement was underway to extend suffrage, the right to vote, to women. By 1893 New Zealand had granted suffrage to all people, by 1918 Britain granted women voting rights and by 1920 the Constitution of the United States had adopted this policy.

Discussion

Do you think that all people are free and equal?

What changes could be made in the future to provide equality for all?

Most communities believe in equality for all people but that is a difficult concept to achieve. What obstacles stand in the way of providing equality for all people?

Research Topics

Constitution of the United States
Martin Luther King, Jr.
Discrimination today

Communities for a New Millennium

Today most of the world lives within a political organization known as the nation-state, a unified geographic area governed by a centralized power to which we all answer. Uprisings, revolutions, democracy and the spread of information have challenged old rules and helped to create the communities we live in today.

Discussion

How is your country or nation-state governed? Who makes decisions? What rights does the average citizen hold?

How is your community linked to the governing of the nation?

What do you like best about your community? What don't you like?

Describe a perfect community. Do you think that such a community could exist?

What role does the family play in a community?

Research Topics

Define the word *community*.
Find out about your country's policies on human rights.
How has the life of children changed in the last 100 years?

Activity

Make a list of all the things that make up a community. Is it just a place or is there more to it?

Make a map of your ideal *Community 2000*. Write a brief description of this community.

Write or draw a sequence of events to describe a typical day in the life of a future family within this community.

Homes for a New Era

Dwellings have come a long way from the bone shelters that early humans built 25,000 years ago.

Discussion

What is the main purpose of a home? What is a typical home in the '90s?

Can everyone live in the kind of home they would like to? Why or why not?

How do the homes we live in affect the natural environment?

Activity

Design your ideal home for the year 2000. Look at real blue-prints, home magazines and books. Consider heating, appliances, wiring and lighting.

Make a model of your home out of cardboard and other found materials.

Research Topics

Castles as dwellings
Modern building materials

Food for the Future

Farming practices began changing during the agricultural revolution when small self-sufficient farming units became part of a large tenancy farm system. In the last century alone we have seen drastic changes in how our food is produced and marketed. Some people predicted that we would be getting all of our nutrients through pills by the year 2000 but that hasn't happened yet, although the food we eat has changed over time.

Discussion

What foods do you like to eat? What do you think are the most popular foods with kids in your age group?

How has the food we eat changed in the last century? How have our eating habits changed over the last century?

In what ways have modern foods improved upon foods of the past?

In what ways are modern foods worse than foods of the past?

Hunger

Some experts believe that the Earth has more than enough resources to feed 11 billion people if the resources are properly managed. Despite this fact, it is believed that between 750 and 950 million people in the world suffer from malnutrition. Poorer nations often lack the resources to grow and harvest food, or they are caught in wars that make it impossible to grow and harvest food. In most of these cases there are no means to bring food to these people.

Activity

Design a farm of the future that makes optimum use of the land and has no harmful effect on the environment.

Devise a plan to ensure that no one goes hungry in the new millennium.

Create a menu for the perfect restaurant of the year 2000 for kids your age.

Plant an organic vegetable garden at your school or in a family garden. Compare your harvest with that of a chemically treated garden.

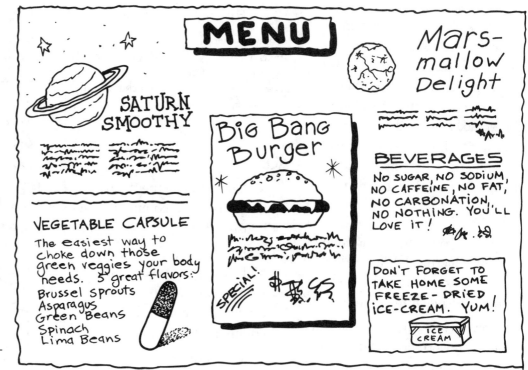

8600 B.C.	First evidence of human farming	
9000 B.C.	Palestinian sheep may be the world's first domesticated animals	
6000 B.C.	Farming spread into Greece, Crete and later into Europe	
900 A.D.	Roman wheeled plows spread throughout the world	

Research Topics

Healthy eating habits
Food additives and agricultural chemicals
Hunger and food banks in your community

Communicating 2000 Style

Early communications were intuitive, verbal or based on visual cues. In time people used symbols, picture writing and eventually written language which emerged c. 3500 B.C. in Sumer, c. 3000 B.C. in Egypt, c. 200 B.C. in Crete and c. 1300 in China. The development of writing was one of the most important events to occur in human history in the last 5000 years. By the 14th century the printing press allowed for the widespread transfer of ideas and information through the printed word. In time communication hit the airwaves as radio; telephone and television opened up communication lines to homes far and wide. Today, people have a world of information and communication at their fingertips through telephone and computer systems that keep us all up-to-date.

Discussion

Try to imagine a world without the printed word. What would it be like?

How did Gutenberg's press affect communication in societies?

What is telecommuting and how might it affect rush hour traffic?

Research Topics

Hieroglyphics
Postal Service
Alexander Graham Bell
Interactive television
Virtual reality
Internet

Activity

Run a printmaking workshop where children can create their own print stamps using sponges, apples or potatoes and paint. Children can cut letters or symbols into their printing device, dip it in paint and say, "start the presses!"

Visit your local newspaper office and find out how information is compiled, printed and spread.

Make use of an age-old form of communication–write a letter!

Design a communication device for the 21st century.

Write the words *Communication Connection* in the center of a bulletin board. Have children turn paper plates into faces and then draw or cut out pictures of devices they use to communicate. Hang the faces and communication devices on the board. Run string between them to illustrate the transfer of information.

c. 15,000 B.C.	Brazilians produce cave art in South America
2000 B.C.	The Sumerian Epic of Gilgamesh recorded on clay tablets is the world's earliest known written story
c. 1040-1050	Movable type is used in China
c. 1450	Gutenberg's press goes into action
1906	First radio program broadcast in the United States
1930	The first television stations hit the airwaves

TLC10109 Copyright © Teaching & Learning Company, Carthage, IL 62321-0010

Getting Around

From the time the wheel was invented, humans have put it to good use. The wheel led to horse-drawn, pedal-powered and eventually steam-powered and motorized vehicles to get us around. Once humans could get around on the ground, they headed for the skies where the first powered flight took place in 1903 and a landing on the moon in 1969.

Discussion

How has the automobile changed the way we live our lives? How has it changed our natural environment?

Do you think that the era of the automobile is good or bad for humanity? Why?

How do you get where you need to go? What methods of transportation are convenient? Which ones are not?

How do you think people will travel in the year 2000? What about the year 3000?

How do means of transportation affect the natural environment? Talk about by-products, paved surfaces, noise and pollution.

Do you know many people who commute long distances to work each day?

Research Topics

Astrolabe
Vehicles over the centuries
Space travel

Activity

Design a dream car for the future. What special features will it have? How will it be powered? Who will buy it?

Design an entirely new method of transportation for the future.

Challenge

When do you think that space travel will be possible for everyone? What barriers might stand in the way of this happening?

c. 3500 B.C.	The Sumerians invent the wheel
c. 3000 B.C.	Egyptians used sailing ships
800-700 B.C.	Horseshoes are used in Europe
c. 350 B.C.	Roads are used in early Rome
c. 1088	The magnetic needle compass is used in China
1869	First transcontinental railroad connects the United States from coast to coast
1903	Wright brothers make their first flight
1912	Henry Ford produces the Model T Ford automobile
1969	*Apollo II* takes U.S. astronauts to the moon

An Apple a Day

Discussion

What do you do to keep yourself healthy? Were these habits always practiced?

How has science helped the health of humanity?

What do you think have been the most important advances in medicine over the last century?

What medical advances can we hope for in the new millennium?

Activity

Write a home remedy prescription for the common cold, a sprained ankle, a bleeding nose or a scraped knee.

Research Topics

International Red Cross
Herbal medicines
Immunization
Florence Nightingale
UNICEF

The 3 Rs and More

From early Greek and Roman times, education has been important–although it was not always available to everyone.

Discussion

Where do you get most of your information? Where do you learn best?

How could schools of the future help children to learn best?

Activity

Write a description of a perfect school in the year 2000.

Describe a typical day in that school.

Research Topics

Education in the 1800s

1796	Edward Jenner invents the first immunization vaccine
1867	Surgical antiseptic invented by Joseph Lister
1895	The X ray invented by Wilhelm Roentgen
1985	World Health Organization declares AIDS to be an epidemic

Let early education be a sort of amusement;
you will then be better able to discover the (child's) natural bent.

Plato, *the Republic*, c. 375 B.C.

Peace, Man; Let's Get Along

Throughout human history there have been conflicts, wars and peaceful resolutions. With advanced technology and powerful weapons, war has become a more and more dangerous prospect. We can only hope that the intellects that could create such devastating weapons will have the intelligence to find peaceful solutions to conflicts.

Discussion

How do you feel when someone does not understand your point of view? How do you help someone to understand your viewpoint?

What do you do when someone else's belief affects your life? Think of situations when this happens in your life: someone wants the baseball diamond when you and your pals are playing ball, someone reads out loud in class and disturbs your work, someone is smoking in your house and it makes it difficult for you to breathe, your little brother or sister shares a room with you and keeps it very messy.

Can you always resolve your problems peacefully? What happens when violence is used to try to solve problems?

Who decides how conflicts are resolved in your country? How can the average citizen make their ideas and opinions heard?

Challenge

How do you think problems will be solved between countries in the future?

Research Topics

United Nations
Mohandas Gandhi
Martin Luther King, Jr.
Nelson Mandela

Activity

Create a "Hand in Hand" bulletin board. Have each child trace and cut out the shape of their hand. On each hand have children write ways that they can find peaceful solutions and walk hand in hand with other beings on the planet.

The longest war in this history of the United States was the Cold War which began at the end of World War II and ended with the collapse of communism in the USSR.
It was a war of words, ideas and fear between the United States and the Soviet Union.

The test of any government is the extent to which it increases the good in the people.

Aristotle, 322 B.C.

Music, Art and Entertainment for a New Millennium

The world has seen many forms of entertainment come and go over the centuries. Some have endured and some have been passing fads. Throughout time every culture has produced its own unique rhythms, instruments and art trends. Music, art and entertainment have been preserved, shared and blended throughout the world to give us the forms that we enjoy today.

Discussion

What kinds of music do you enjoy listening to or playing?

What forms of entertainment have endured throughout the centuries?

What new forms of entertainment can we expect in the new millennium?

What new kinds of artwork are being made today?

What new types of artwork might we see in the future?

Activity

Write and perform a live play about the year 2000.

Design a musical instrument that may be used in the future.

Visit a local art gallery or museum.

Study a famous artist and produce your own artwork in that particular style.

Research Topics

Troubadours of the 1100s and 1200s
Shakespeare's Globe Theater
Michelangelo
Claude Monet
Academy Awards
Group of Seven Artists

200-100 B.C.	Flutes and panpipes played in Latin America
c. 500 B.C.	First theaters were built in Greece
1000 A.D.	Guido d'Arezzo invents staff notation
1508-1512	Michelangelo painted ceiling of Sistine Chapel in Rome
c. 1585	Shakespeare began career in London theater
c. 1700	The piano is invented
1742	First performance of Handel's *Messiah* in Dublin
1869	First exhibition of Impressionist painting in Paris
1877	Thomas Edison invented the phonograph
1890s	Jazz was born in the city of New Orleans
1895	First public screening of a movie in Paris
1927	First talking film, *The Jazz Singer*, released
1913	Hollywood becomes center of movie industry
1950	Rock and Roll becomes popular
1956	Elvis Presley makes his first U.S. hit–"Heartbreak Hotel"
1982	First CDs go on sale
1996	*Cats* becomes the longest running musical in history of Broadway

Just for Fun

Since the beginning of time, people have amused themselves with pastimes, playthings and style.

Discussion

What playthings are popular with you and your pals today?

What toys do you think might be available to children in the year 2000?

Activity

Invent a toy that will take the play world by storm in the new millennium.

Research Topics

How did your parents and grandparents pass their leisure time?

What can you find out about Silly Putty®?

3000 B.C.	Marbles are used in Egypt
400 B.C.	Yo-yos and kites are played with in ancient China
300 A.D.	Mayans play with hard rubber balls
1903	Crayola® wax crayons were invented
1945	Slinky was invented
1957	Frisbee™ is manufactured and sold as the "Pluto Platter"
1959	Barbie doll appears on the runway
1966	Twister™ game gets kids and adults twisting
1975	The video game is launched in Japan
1984	BMX™ bikes become popular in Britain
1990	Nintendo™ hits the market

Fashion Fads for the Future

Although kids don't always care what they wear, there have been definite fashion trends on the playgrounds for centuries.

Discussion

What fashion items are hot right now? What makes some styles popular?

How do *you* decide what you like and don't like to wear?

Which fashion trends do you think will survive into the next century?

Activity

What new fashion trends might we expect in the 2000s? Design for the future!

Provide cardboard cut-outs to be dressed for the future: cloth, colored paper, coloring materials, glitter and glue for the fashions.

Research Topics

How has fashion changed since your parents or grandparents were kids?

How are the clothes you wear made?

Travel Destination: Space!

Travelers who have conquered mountains, been on safari and cruised the oceans blue will be looking for new travel destinations in the near future. There is a new frontier just waiting to be explored–space! Soon you might be able to commute to the moon for a holiday. Believe it or not the first space tours are thought to take place in about the year 2022! The workings for such travel have not yet been put in place but plans are in the making.

Space touring vehicles will be reliable, reusable rockets designed to hold at least 50 travelers. The vehicle will need large windows for viewing space. Passengers may take a trip into space and back, around the Earth excursion or possibly travel into space for an extended stay in space hotel–the blueprints have already been prepared! The cost of travel to this tourist hot spot will be out of this world but for those who can afford it–Bon voyage!

Activity

Design a travel brochure for the Space Vacation Tourism Industry.

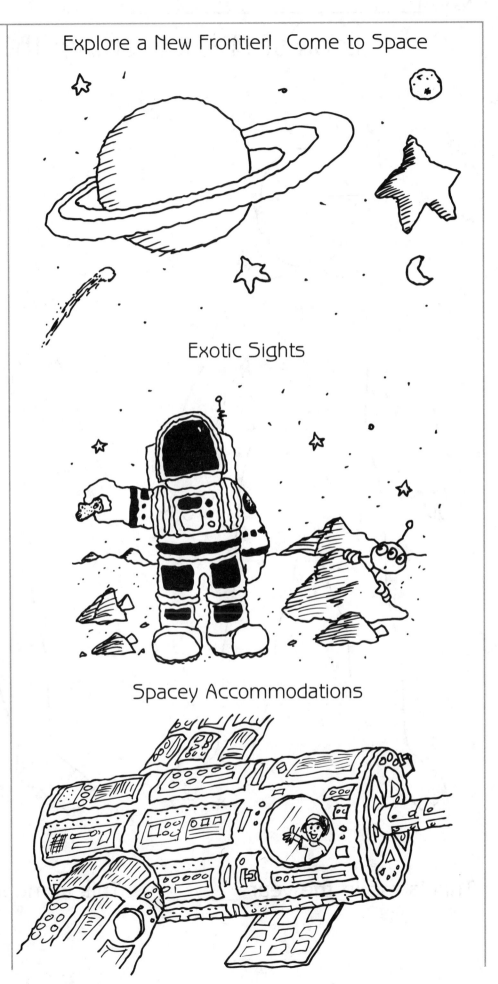

Explore a New Frontier! Come to Space

Exotic Sights

Spacey Accommodations

Name _____

Look at Me Now and in the Future!

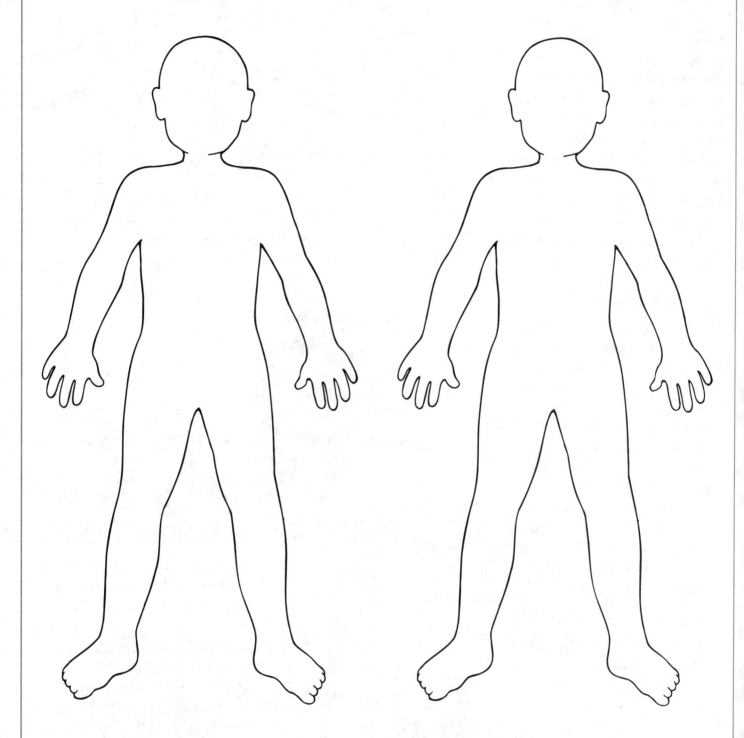

This is me in the year _____.   This is me in the year _____.

Footsteps into the Future

Encourage children to think about their goals in life and the means they have to achieve these goals.

Materials

construction paper

drawing and writing instruments

scissors

Get Ready

1. Ask each child to think about where they would like to see themselves in the future. What would they like to be doing? Where would they like to be living? What kind of person would they like to be?

What to Do

1. Have children trace both of their feet onto the construction paper.

2. Children cut out the tracings of both feet.

3. On the first "foot" children will write about ways they can achieve the goals, lifestyle and personal styles they desire. Talk about schooling, work habits, volunteer service, relaxation, fitness level, skill development, friendships, financial planning, guidance and assistance services that will help them to become the kind of person they want to be.

5. On the second "foot" children write about the ways they will make their goals and aspirations come true.

Bulletin Board Idea

Create a letter board or banner that reads *Footsteps into the Future*.

Place their pairs of footprints around or leading away from this title.

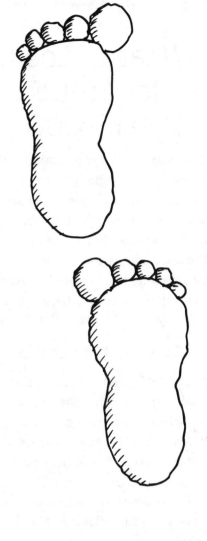

Recognize the Class of 2000

The class of a particular year usually refers to the graduating year; however, on this special occasion everyone can be a class of 2000. Your group can be the _____ grade Class of 2000. Make a Class of 2000 Yearbook with insights about the past and predictions for the future. The All About Me! on page 33 can be included in your yearbook.

What to Look for in the Year 2000

The year 2000 is just around the corner, and it's sure to be a banner year! Everyone is riding the wave of enthusiasm. Exciting events on land, in the sea and in the sky and space will make this a year to remember–even if it didn't have all those zeros! Let's take a peek at what the year 2000 holds.

Celestial Happenings

Even the heavens will mark this date. Head for the hills with your telescope, binoculars or your naked eye. The new millennium will be marked in the skies by a lunar eclipse on January 20, 2000–the first in North American skies since the eclipse of March 1997.

Activity

Draw diagrams to show what happens during an eclipse.

Chinese Year of the Dragon

In Chinese culture, the year that you are born is as important as the day you arrive. Each year is designated by one of 12 animal signs. The year that you are born determines your animal sign. The year 2000 will be the year of the Dragon.

Activity

Write a story about a child born under the sign of the dragon. What characteristics might you expect from those born under this sign?

Computer Chaos

Computers are marvels that can do many things–but unfortunately many computers we use today won't be able to correctly read the year 2000. They just weren't programmed to do it. No one thought that the operating systems of the '60s would still be here when the new millennium arrived, so the computers weren't trained to read the date 2000. Many fear that this will lead to a period of computer chaos.

Experts believe that the United States may experience "massive disruptions" in many critical areas. Many federal agency computers assume that all of the first two digits in a date are 19. These computers will read "00" and assume the year is 1900. That's sure to cause some confusion!

Of course teams of programmers are already trying to remedy this problem. Unfortunately, many of the programs were written in '60s computer languages that few programmers know today. Those who do know how to fix the problem are faced with hours and hours of programming changes. Estimates say that correcting this little problem may cost anywhere between 2.3 and 10 billion dollars in the U.S. alone. The worldwide costs have been estimated at 1.5 trillion U.S. dollars. That's a lot of tax dollars! At this time only a few federal agencies have realistic plans to solve this problem before the year 2000 arrives.

Activity

Check the newspapers, magazines and the internet to find out how the world is doing at handling this problem.

Olympic Year

The Games of the XXVIIth Olympiad will take place in Sydney, Australia, in the year 2000. Olympics 2000 is expected to draw more than 10,000 athletes from 171 nations. Athletes are training to be in top form, and spectators will scramble for tickets and accommodations for this millennium Olympics.

Activity

Research the history of the Olympic Games. How has it changed since it began?

What could make the first Olympics of the new millennium outstanding?

Host a Mini Olympics 2000 of your own.

Leap Year 2000

Since everything else seems to be happening this year, it's no surprise that the leap year came around for the occasion.

Activity

Find out how this four-year cycle got started and why.

Earth Day 2000

Over 300 million people worldwide are expected to participate in Earth Day 2000. This will be the thirtieth Earth Day since this meaningful occasion was created.

Activity

Host an Earth Day celebration to honor the Earth on this important date. Plant a tree to remind you of your pledge to care for the Earth.

Mayflower 2000

In the spring of 1999, an experienced crew and some adventurous passengers will set sail for the New World on *Mayflower 2000*.

Activity

Write a story from the perspective of a passenger on the original *Mayflower*.

Holy Year of Jubilee

Christians will be celebrating the 2000th birthday of their savior Jesus Christ and the traditional Holy Year of Jubilee. It is a year of liberation, reconciliation, justice, peace, celebration and joy. This special event occurs every 50 years to remind Christians to honor God by showing respect, equality and justice for all.

One definition for the whole millennia refers to the thousand years mentioned in the Book of Revelation 20, during which holiness is to triumph and Christ will reign the Earth. Throughout history Christian people have expected the Second Coming of Christ to occur at the end of a thousand-year period.

Activity

Do one small act of kindness this year in the name of peace.

Astronomers have noted that on September 15, 7 B.C.
a rare conjunction of the planets Jupiter and Saturn appeared as a huge star in the sky which may have accounted for the star of Bethlehem, which would have made September 15, 1993, the 2000th birthday of Jesus.

THE ROOM-CLEANING ROBOT

The Future Is Here!

Many expected the world to be a very different place by the year 2000. Some expected sensible things to happen and others anticipated unusual futuristic phenomena. Some expectations have come to pass and others have not.

Ideas for the Future

Leonardo da Vinci (1452-1519) was a great thinker whose ideas were centuries ahead of his time. He was one of the most remarkable inventors, architects, engineers, scientists, writers *and* mathematicians the world has *ever* known. Da Vinci worked on mechanical sketches for inventions including the self-propelled vehicle, the steam engine, submarine, paddle boat, driver's helmet, parachute and helicopter. He even explained the workings of the human heart almost 500 years before modern scientists were able to do so.

Research

Investigate some of Da Vinci's inventions.

Time Travel

Some people thought that time travel might be possible by the year 2000. Now that we're here you might say we traveled through time–but we did it all in good time–moving the usual way from the past to the present and on into the future with no control over that passage through time.

Some people believe that time travel might someday be possible through an understanding of science and technology, while others believe it is possible now by tapping into the powers and mysteries of the universe.

Discussion

Have you ever wanted to travel into the future? If you could do it, what year would you travel to? Where would you visit? Would you want to visit a space colony or see Earth itself? What do you think would await you in that time?

Challenge

Do you think that time travel will ever be possible? Why or why not?

Space Colonies

Many people speculated that there would be colonies in space by the year 2000, and they were right! We have set up experimental colonies floating in space for periods of time, and who knows where that research might take us. NASA has plans for a space station to be sent to Mars sometime after the year 2000. Although space stations are a reality in this era of space exploration, we haven't yet started to colonize the universe the way people had predicted.

Challenge

Design a colony that could support thousands of people in space.

Robot Control

Many forward thinkers predicted that robots would do much of our work for us by the year 2000. We have technological helpers to wash our cars, wash our dishes, clean our clothes, answer our telephones and make everything imaginable in manufacturing plants. These machines do much of our work for us but haven't tried to take over the world as some science fiction writers proposed.

Activity

Design a robot for the future to do anything you want.

UFOs

Have you checked the skies lately? Some people expected us to have made contact with UFOs (Unidentified Flying Objects, that is) by the year 2000. Some people claim to have seen strange flying objects in the sky and no explanation can be found for the sightings–that is of course why they are called *unidentified* flying objects!

Science Meets Fiction

Science fiction is a form of writing that combines elements of science with elements of the imagination. Scientific facts are exaggerated to various degrees to create fictional tales of a possible future. Some early science fiction writers used this technique to create futuristic scenarios that actually came to pass.

Discussion

Have you ever seen a strange sight in the night sky? What was it? What conditions can make lights look unusual? What do you think about UFOs? Do you think that spaceships could come from outer space and visit Earth?

Activity

Interview an alien! Pretend that you are the first reporter on the scene of a UFO landing. Interview the alien beings. What does the alien look like, how does the being communicate and how did it end up on our planet? What knowledge could an alien share with us earthlings? What could we share with an alien?

Activity

Write your own science fiction story combining scientific facts from your knowledge and fantasy facts from your imagination.

One famous science fiction writer whose fiction came to be fact was Jules Verne. In his book *Journey from the Earth to the Moon*, written in 1865, Verne predicted that rockets would be launched from Florida and that animals would be sent on test flights–both scenarios became fact. In his book *20,000 Leagues Under the Sea*, written in 1870, Verne wrote about an underwater ship that inspired the first submarine 28 years later.

Activity

Tap into your imagination to create a vehicle for a science fiction story.

Speculation

Many people, including writers, have speculated about what might happen in the future. There have been many tales of space travel, visits from aliens and travels through time. An English writer by the name of H.G. Wells wrote about time travel and an invasion of the Earth by beings from Mars. The last two scenarios created quite a stir but have not come to pass . . . yet.

Discussion

Do you believe that there could be other beings somewhere in the universe?

Predictions for the Future

The year 2000 seems to have captured the imaginations of people for, well, about a millennium. Everyone wonders what the new millennium will bring, and some people even try to foretell what will be. This futuristic year has been the target of much speculation and prediction. Some predictions were made a long, long time ago by prophets–people believed to have the ability to foresee the future.

Discussion

What movies and books are most popular right now? Do you think that these topics may be related to millennium mania?

CHANNEL 150 WEATHER
TONIGHT'S FORECAST

A well-known prophet named Nostradamus lived in France in the 1500s. His prophecies were made through poetic riddles that were to be solved by the people who lived in the particular eras foretold. There is some disagreement regarding the translations as well as the meaning of Nostradamus' riddles. However, many believe that his prophecies ring true. One of his most well-known prophecies for this millennium reads something like this:

> The year 1999/
> month seven/
> From the sky/
> shall come a great/
> king of terror.

No one knows exactly what Nostradamus is referring to. Do you have any ideas?

This millennium year will no doubt attract more doomsday prophecies . . . but don't get concerned. These sort of predictions come and go when there's an important year. The end of the world has been predicted many times and in spite of the worry such predictions caused, nothing ever came to pass.

Scientific Predictions

Scientists make predictions with the information they gather from scientific research and observations. Scientists make predictions all of the time based on a scientific method of observation, analysis, forming of a hypothesis and testing. Scientists make changes and run the experiments over and over until they have what is called a proven theory which they then use to make predictions about everything from the weather to human health. Scientific predictions are based on solid ground and are often correct . . . but not always. We are always rediscovering truths.

Activity

Predict and Seal

Turn your thoughts to the future. Have each participant write predictions for the coming year and then seal these in a self-addressed envelope. Collect the envelopes and save them to be mailed to the "prophets" in one year's time.

Predictions for a New Millennium

Although you probably don't know what will happen in the future, you can make some predictions based upon what you know about the past and the present. Complete the following with your insights about the future.

In the new millennium I predict that . . .

children will spend more time _____

_____

schools will _____

_____

many children my age will grow up to _____

_____

parents will _____

_____

people will travel by _____

our systems of communicating will _____

_____

farms and rural areas will _____

_____

highways and freeways will _____

_____

our water resources will _____

_____

our air will _____

_____

our natural environment will _____

_____

Name _____

This Is Me in the Year 2000

Care to travel to the future? Although we can't know for sure what the year 2000 will bring, we *can* make predictions.

In the year 2000 . . .

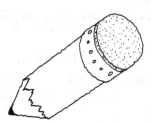

I will be _____ years old and be in grade _____

I will live _____

I will have _____ hair.

I will have _____ sisters and _____ brothers.

I will spend my time _____

My favorite kind of music will be _____

I will be responsible for _____

_____

My town will change by _____

_____

The biggest difference in my life will be that _____

_____

The biggest difference in the world will be _____

_____

Name _____

A Day in the Year 2000

Date: _____

Dear Diary,

The **2000** TIMES

Hot New Band Steals the Fans

_____
_____
_____
_____
_____
_____
_____
_____

Eat at _____

Don't forget to try our new _____.

Shoppers World
SALE
Extravaganza

Don't Miss This Weekend's
Sale of the Century!

_____
_____
_____
_____
_____
_____
_____
_____
_____
_____
_____

The _____
Makes a Comeback!

_____
_____
_____
_____
_____

PLAYING TONIGHT
_____
_____

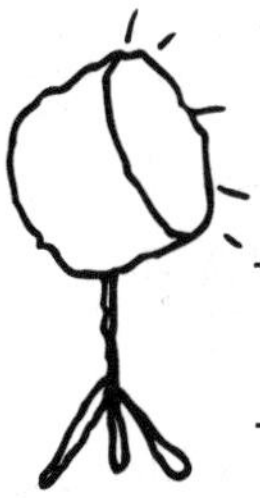

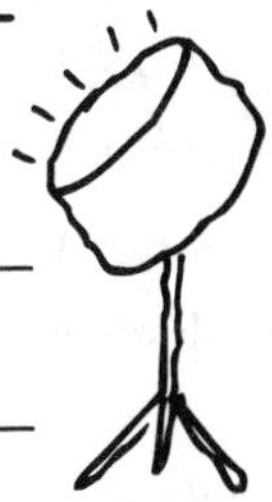

Kids Fight to Save

_____
_____
_____

Sports Fans Leap for Joy When . . .

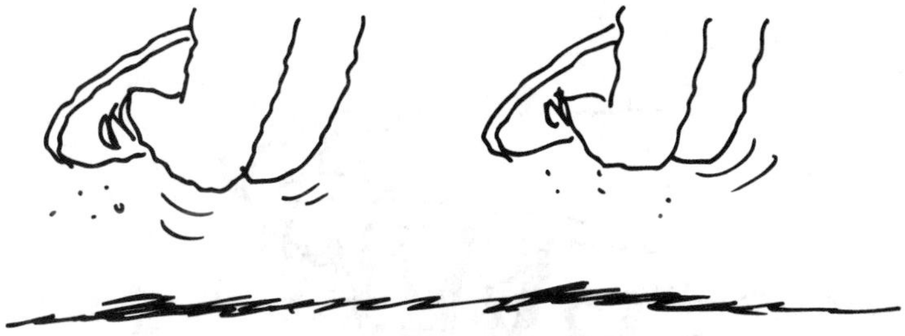

_____
_____
_____
_____
_____

_____
_____
_____
_____

Voyage Through the Millennia with Books

Take children on a journey through the ages from the year 1 A.D. to the dawn of the third millennium with a reading voyage through the last millennium. Young readers can join the voyage and read their way through the centuries. These adventures in reading will bring the past, present and future alive for children of the new millennium. Books will take readers to the heart of the times where children's imaginations can be activated and their knowledge expanded.

Ask your librarian and other book lovers to help you establish a collection of books for your reading journey. Mark the books with a special millennium reading symbol to flag the special voyage selections.

Suggested Readings

1 A.D. to 999 A.D.

The Lost Wreck of the Isis by Robert D. Ballard, Madison Press, 1990.

An exciting look at an ancient Roman vessel and the adventures of those who sailed it about 355 A.D.

The Kingfisher Book of The Ancient World: From the Ice Age to the Fall of Rome by Hazel Mary Martell, Kingfisher, 1995.

A richly detailed exploration of all aspects of the ancient world.

The Middle Ages; 1000 to 1490 A.D.

The Midwife's Apprentice by Karen Kushman, Houghton Mifflin, 1995.

A captivating tale of a homeless, nameless girl who makes a life for herself in medieval England.

The Pied Piper of Hamelin by Michele Lemieux, Kids Can Press/Morrow Junior, 1995.

1284 tale of medieval Germany and the rats that brought chaos.

Waiting for u: The Life of Renaissance Architect Filippo Brunelleschi by Michael Bender and Michael Raincoast, Chronicle Books, 1995.

Young Joan by Barbara Dana, HarperCollins/Charlotte Zolotow Books, 1991.

A moving tale of the life of the French heroine, Joan of Arc.

15th and 16th Centuries

Morning Girl by Michael Dorris. Hyperion Books for Children, 1992.

Readers enter the world of 12-year-old Morning Girl and her brother Star Boy on a Caribbean island in 1492–a world that we know will be altered when Morning Girl discovers a canoeful of strange visitors.

Bartholomew Fair by Mary Stolz, Greenwillow Books/Beech Tree Books, 1990.

A romp through a London fair in 1597 offered from various perspectives.

17th Century

Saturnalia by Paul Fleischman, HarperKeypoint/Charlotte Zolotow Books, 1992.

A look at life from the perspective of a 14-year-old Narragansett Indian in Boston in 1681.

Only Brave Tomorrows by Binifred Bruce Luhrmann, Houghton Mifflin, 1989.

A 1600s tale of a young Faith Ralston, an immigrant from England who is the lone survivor of an Indian massacre in a Massachusetts colony.

18th Century

My Name Is Not Angelica by Scott O'Dell, Dell/Yearling Books, 1990.

A moving tale set in 1733, of a 16-year-old African girl and her betrothed, an African tribal chief, who are sold into slavery.

The Sioux by Virginia Driving Hawk Sneve, illustrated by Ronald Himler, Holiday House, 1995.

A history of the Sioux people and their harrowing migrations to the Plains in the 1700s.

19th Century

A Pioneer Story: The Daily Life of a Canadian Family in 1840 by Barbara Greenwood, illustrated by Heather Collins, Kids Can Press/Tricknor and Fields, 1994.

A highly detailed historical look at pioneer life on a backwoods farm.

Kiersten, an American Girl by Janet Shaw, Pleasant Company Publications, 1986.

The American Girl Collection offers five series about girls from different time periods throughout American history. This series tells the story of a young Swedish girl who reaches the shores of America on a small ship in 1854.

On the Mayflower, Voyage of the Ship's Apprentice and of a Passenger Girl by Kate Waters, photographs by Russ Kendall, Scholastic Inc., 1996.

The story of a bond of friendship that forms on an important historical journey is told with text and photographs of the *Mayflower II.*

Shades of Gray by Carolyn Reeder, Macmillan, 1989.

The tale of a 12-year-old boy orphaned by the Civil War who is adopted by an uncle who refused to fight and is seen as a traitor by his new adoptee.

20th Century

Ragtime Tumpie by Alan Schroeder, illustrations by Bernie Guchs; Little, Brown, 1989.

A fictional biography of entertainer Josephine Baker in the 1915 St. Louis ragtime scene.

Number the Stars by Lois Lowry, Houghton, 1989.

A story of tension and friendship set in World War II in Denmark when the Danes defend their Jewish neighbors.

Just Like New by Anislie Manson, illustrations by Karen Reczuch, Groundwood/Douglas & McIntyre, 1995.

Christmas tale of giving set in 1940s war-torn England.

Angel Square by Brian Doyle, Groundwood, 1984.

A timely book of tolerance and understanding of cultural differences centered in Ottawa, Canada.

Forbidden City by William Bell, Doubleday, 1990.

A compelling tale of heroism set in the 1989 student uprising in Tian An Men Square.

21st Century and Beyond

Time Ghost by Welwyn Wilton Katz, Groundwood/Douglas & McIntyre, 1994.

An exciting 21st century time travel tale of relationships and responsibilities for the care of the Earth.

The Riddle of the Stones and Other Unsolved Mysteries by Daniel Cohen, illustrations by Peter Dennis, Kingfisher, 1995.

This book of real-life mysteries ties the newest generation to perplexing mysteries that have been with people for some time.

The Tower to the Sun by Colin Thompson, Knopf, 1997.

A poignant future fable rich with illustrative detail and message.

Name _____

Voyage Through the Millennia

Join the voyage! Read your way through the centuries and record your travels below.

Time Period	Book Title	Date of Journey

Chapter 6: Ring in a New Millennium!

A significant year such as the year 2000 calls for celebration, contemplation and change in our lives. It signifies the end of an old era and the dawn of the future.

It's time for bangers and clangers, bells and rattles, party hats, streamers and countdowns! It's time for the New Year's celebration of a lifetime. Although the new millennium officially rings in on January 1, 2001–the big celebrations are going to be held December 31, 1999, and into January 1, 2000. The countdown of the millennium is already on, and it's time to start planning your celebration of the century.

Although every culture does it in their own way, almost everyone seems to mark the end of the old year and welcome the new. The new year is seen as a time to reflect on the past, dream for the future and have fun!

New Year 2000 won't be like any other celebration we have seen in this . . . well, millennium! The dawning of the new millennium will bring with it a sense of newness and hope for the future that will be reflected in festivities all over the world. All of the western world will be caught up in the excitement of this occasion and there will be celebrations just about everywhere.

Although New Year's Day is one of our oldest holidays, it hasn't always been celebrated on January 1. In fact New Year's Day was celebrated even before there was a January 1! The month of January didn't exist until Julius Caesar created the new calendar in the 1st century B.C.

Discussion

How do you celebrate the new year? Will your traditional celebration differ for the year 2000?

Does the year 2000 hold any special meaning for you?

What makes this year special for you?

How will you make this year different from any other?

Millennium Mania

Activity

Start a collection of bells to ring in the new year. Use these for math, art and music activities before the official ringing.

Make a list of the top 20 ways you can think of to celebrate the great date.

Make up a millennium phrase.

Make up cryptograms for the word *millennium*.

Decorate a tree with party hats, streamers, horns and printed wishes for the year.

Make your own party hats.

Challenge

How old will you be when you celebrate the year 2000?

Countdown to 2000

Make the countdown to the new millennium a lasting memory!

The magic hour that everyone counts down to is 12:00 a.m. People start getting enthusiastic and excited about 11:58 and prepare for the countdown of seconds.

If your group can't be together to celebrate the magic hour, why not stage it a little early? Then you can celebrate twice! You can create the scene with a large calendar page for the month of December and a large clock. A wizard's cloak and hat or a little magic (sparkle) dust to sprinkle around the clock and calendar can set the stage for your quick trip through the days.

Invite the children to join you on a journey through time that will take you ahead in time: _____ days and _____ hours. (The kids can help you to figure out the exact zoom through time you need!)

When you have reached December 31, 1999, 11:00 or so, you are ready to start celebrating. All eyes will be on the clock throughout the party–awaiting the magnificent millennium countdown. Start the countdown chorus at 11:59 and be prepared for enthusiasm!

The 21st century (or 2000th year of our calendar) really begins on January 1, in the year 2001. In that year we can say that our calendar began 2000 years ago. Many people will be celebrating the year 2000 anyway. When will you count down to a new millennium?

How Will You Celebrate?

There is a wide world of possibilities for celebrating the important date–you can do just about anything–but chances are you will want to do something special to make this occasion memorable.

Parties are already being organized in cities, towns, villages and homes just about everywhere. Millennium masquerades and charity balls, beach parties and festivals of all sorts are already in the works. If you want to party, you're sure to find company. Some people want to travel and plans for special trips are already underway. You may have trouble finding a quiet place to celebrate because it seems that things will be hopping come 12 midnight wherever you go!

Where Will You Celebrate?

Celebrations will be occurring just about everywhere around the world. Some large cities are keeping their Celebration 2000 plans quiet for now, so we will all be surprised by the proceedings when they occur. Some countries, cities and organizations are going public with all the details and looking for participants. Reservations are already fully booked at some destinations and for some events at home and around the world.

Where are people celebrating? You'll find New Year 2000 revelers on the sea, land and air, on beaches, boats, mountain peaks and horseback and, of course, the city streets.

Millennium Mania Celebrations

The biggest bash in recent history is going to be celebrated with vigor around the world when the year 2000 arrives. Ships will sail, planes will fly, Concords will jet, fireworks and bonfires will light up the sky, concerts will rock, adventurers will travel, tours will be underway and celebrations will take off.

Discussion

Where would you like to be and what would you like to be doing when the clock strikes midnight for the first time in the year 2000?

Many years from now when someone asks, "Where were you when the clock struck 12 in the year 2000?" will you remember?

GET READY, EVERYONE... HERE IT COMES!

Although some people will stay at home or visit friends, many people are already making big plans for the millennium celebrations. People want to be somewhere memorable or do something memorable for the big date. Believe it or not, many events have already been sold out! Trips, tours, parties, concerts and some hotels are no longer taking reservations. Disney World hotels, Millennium Cruises and many hotels in desirable locations are already sold out for December 31, 1999.

Many events are already claiming to be "The World's Largest New Year's Eve Party." We'll just have to wait until the day after to know for sure where the distinction will go!

The first North American city to greet the year 2000 will be the town of St. John's in the Canadian province of Newfoundland.

Activity

Find St. John's on your globe.

There will be millennium celebrations on the Golden Gate Bridge in San Francisco, at the Great Wall of China and, of course, at Times Square in New York City—just to mention a few locations! Some people are going to follow the new year around the world and fly through the time zones on a Concord jet as the millennium draws near.

It is quite an honor to have the first light of the new millennium shine on you–and a few places are claiming this great sunrise! Experts seem to agree that a change made to the location of the international date line in 1994 makes Caroline Island of Kiribati in the central Pacific Ocean the place where this millennium sunrise will occur. At 6:05 a.m. Greenwich Mean Time, the sun's rays will reach the island, but few people will see it as this island has very few inhabitants. The neighboring Kiribati island of Christmas will be the first populated place where the sunrise will be witnessed by people–this is expected to occur at 6:29 a.m. GMT.

Many places will celebrate the first light on the dawn of the year 2000, even if they aren't the first to catch the rays!

While many people will welcome the new year with spectacular celebrations, others will meet the millennium in quiet reflection, spiritual ceremony, communion with nature or by sleeping through the whole affair!

Traditions for 2000

Everyone has their own way of celebrating. In many countries New Year's Day is a national holiday and people celebrate on New Year's Eve with small gatherings of friends and family; religious ceremonies or extravagant galas with music, noise and a round of midnight kisses. Many of our new year's rituals have been with us for a long time and will follow us into another millennium.

Find a Coin

Find the coin in the cake and have good luck for the year to come. In an old Greek tradition, *peta* or *Vassilopitta* cake is baked with a gold or silver coin in it. The person who is served the coin gets luck for the year–or in this case, maybe millennium!

Eat a Pea

Eat a pea and gain a dollar! In the southern United States, it is believed that the number of black-eyed peas you eat on New Year's Day will predict the number of dollars you will earn in the year to come. Many people cook and eat them on this day . . . just in case the superstition is true!

Put the First Foot Through the Doorway

The first person through the front door after the midnight hour is called the "first-footer." The first-footer is seen as an omen as to what kind of luck the household can expect in the coming year. Tall, black-haired men bearing a gift of some sort foretell of much good fortune in the coming year. Often this type of visitor is set up to be the first to step through the door.

Join the Parade

Chinese people living in large cities outside of China host spectacular parades with large colorful dragons and noisy fireworks to usher in the new year. The color red is considered good luck and is very popular at these new year celebrations.

Get a Fresh Start

In many cultures around the world, people put their lives in order before the new year arrives. Homes are cleaned, debts are paid and wrongs are made right.

Noodles for Life

At the new year, traditional Japanese families eat *soba*, a kind of buckwheat noodle that symbolizes long life.

Activity

Start a new tradition of your own.

First Night Celebrations

A combination of old celebrations is being made new again in many cities across North America in First Night Celebrations. Create your own special celebration to ring in the new millennium using the suggestions below.

Light Up the Night

Hang festive lights to illuminate your celebration.

Have a Parade

Children can dress to represent elements from their own cultural celebrations of the new year. Painted faces, costumes and props can bring the various customs to life.

Water Ballet

In towns with canals, rivers or other waterways, people can look forward to splendid floating displays of lighted water parades and boat ballets.

POSSIBLE MASCOTS FOR THE NEW MILLENNIUM

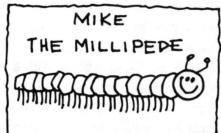

MIKE THE MILLIPEDE

"2K" THE KOALA

TECHNO 2000 FUTURE GUY

MILLIE METER — BRAINS AND BEAUTY

Millennium Mascot

The name *millipede* means "thousand feet." Even though millipedes really have only about 400 feet, they have become popular recently. Create a year 2000 creature, character or mascot to represent the year. Draw it, make models or dress up like your mascot.

Flag the New Millennium

Design a flag to represent the new millennium. Make up a slogan, anthem or pledge to go with it.

Countdown to a Crazy Toss

Prepare to toss caution to the wind when the clock strikes 12. Get ready to throw grass seed, birdseed, popcorn, peanuts or other biodegradable treats for the Earth.

Celebration Supper

Get together with friends for a celebration supper. A potluck affair would allow everyone to contribute a special celebratory delicacy.

Sun Watch: Track the Last Sunset and the First Light

Watch the sun set on the old millennium and then awake in time to watch the first light of the new millennium.

Challenge

How many sunrises and sunsets do you have behind you?

Name That Decade

What should we call the first decade in the 21st century? We've had the '80s and '90s–what's next?

Through the Door to a New Millennium

1. Cut along the dotted lines so you can open your doors.

2. Put glue along the back of the page everywhere but on the door.

3. Paste this page on top of another blank page. When you open the doors, you will see blank paper behind the doors.

4. Write the year that is ending on one door and the new year on the other. Decorate the doors.

5. Draw things behind the first door that remind you of the old year. Draw things behind the new year door that you expect and hope to see in the new year.

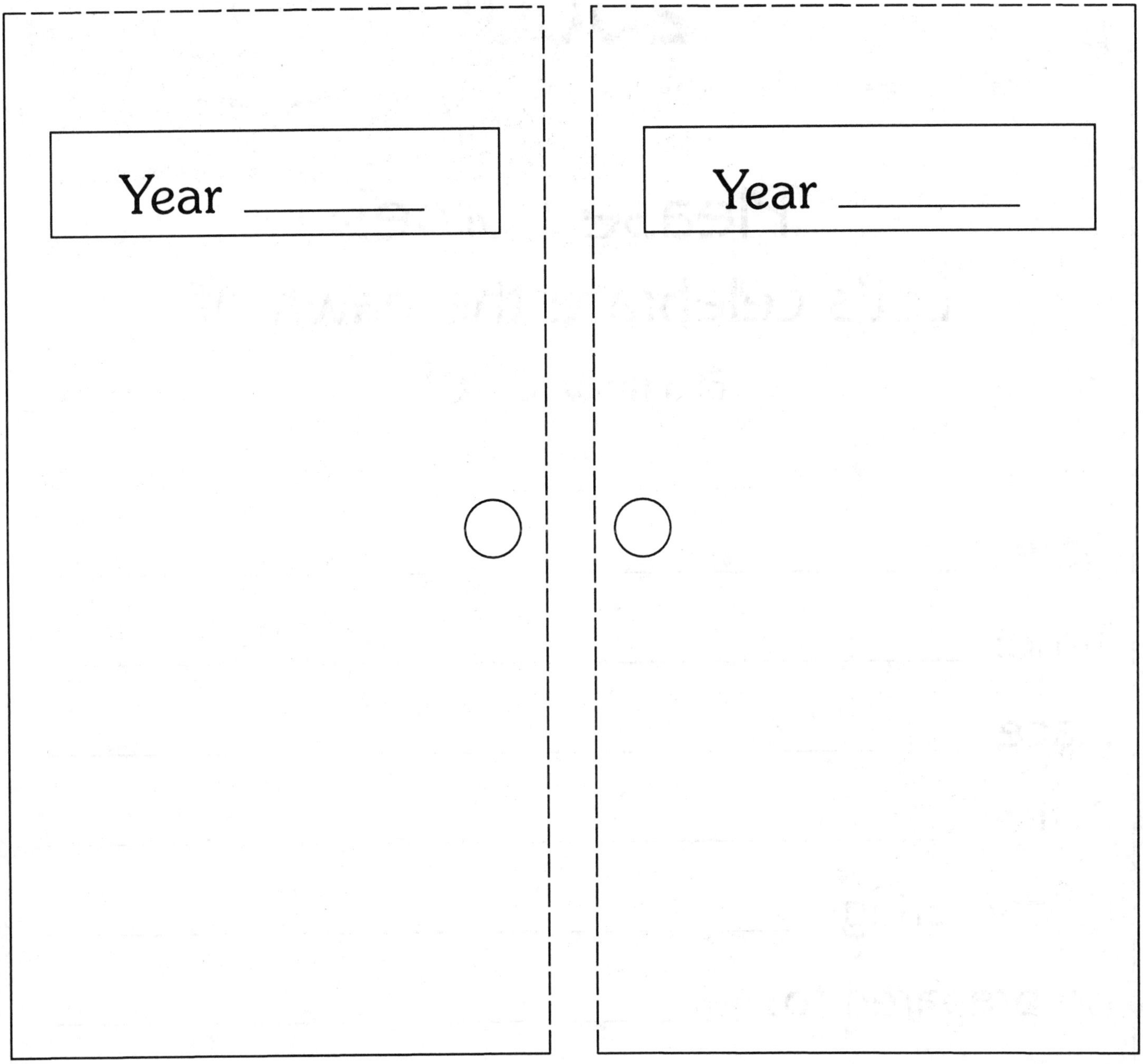

Year _____

Year _____

Host Your Personal Party of the Century

Ring in the millennium with personal pizzazz. Be it a big bash or a quiet walk in the woods, plan the where, what, when, who and hows of your big bash! Make an invitation to invite friends and fill them in on all the details. Complete and decorate the invitation below.

Celebrate the Year 2000!

Please come!
Let's celebrate the dawn of a new age!

Date: _____

Time: _____

Place: _____

Attire: _____

Please bring: _____

Be prepared to: _____

Listen to the New Year!

If you were to walk around your town on New Year's Eve, chances are you'll hear people celebrating all over town. Many of these noisemaking traditions came from a belief that making noise as the new year arrived would ward off evil spirits for that coming year.

When the Clock Strikes 12, You Might Hear . . .

your Scottish neighbors banging pots and pans.

Chilean neighbors celebrating with a round of their national anthem.

the bells of the Buddhist temple toll 108 times.

French Canadian celebrators singing and entertaining in a door-to-door tradition.

people from all cultures counting down to the second and greeting the new year with cheers, noise, songs and kisses.

revelers from all over the world joining in the chorus of what is probably the most famous song of the new year–"Auld Lang Syne" written by Scottish Poet Robert Burns.

Make Some Noise!

You can make your own bangers, clangers, shakers and ringers to ring in the new year! Get creative with recycled materials and ring in the new year with enthusiasm. With a little effort you can turn those shakers into a new year's welcoming band with songs to accompany the rhythm.

Shakers

Materials

clear plastic containers (water bottles look great!)

brightly colored beans, beads, buttons and marbles

electrical tape

What to Do

1. Fill the bottle about $1^1/2$ full with the dried materials.
2. Seal the lid with electrical tape.
3. Shake your way into the new year.

Drum Up Some Enthusiasm

Materials

tin or cardboard round containers with plastic lids

colored pencils or painted dowel rods about $1/4"$ (.6 cm) in diameter

construction paper or peel and stick vinyl

markers, paint or stickers

What to Do

1. Decorate the exterior of the drum with construction paper or peel and stick vinyl, stickers and paint or markers.
2. Replace the cover on the container.
3. Make drumsticks by wrapping the ends of colored pencils with masking tape until you have a wad that looks like a ball.

Resolutions

The new year is a time to reflect over the past and look forward to the future. It is a time to change old ways into better ways. From ancient times people have used the dawn of a new year as a time to make changes in their lives. People like to set goals for themselves or vow to make changes or improvements over the coming year. These vows are called new year's resolutions–you may have heard about them. Every year is a new year with opportunities just waiting for us if we are prepared to reach for them. Resolutions help us to think about what is important to us, what we want and how to resolve problems and accomplish the things we want to. Simple resolutions are the easiest to keep and can put us on the right track to greater changes in our lives.

Make Some Resolutions of Your Own

Just Do It!

Is there something that you have always wanted to do but couldn't? Ask yourself why you haven't done it, what steps you need to take to be able to do it and then resolve to do it! How about running a mile; reading a good book; speaking a new language; playing an instrument; saying "hi" to a new friend; writing a story; cleaning up your room; learning to swim, riding a bike, in-line skating or playing tennis. You can do whatever you want to do . . . just resolve to do it!

Help Out

Have you always wanted to do something for someone else but weren't sure how to go about it? Resolve to help out this year–you'll feel better and so will the people you help. Share your talents with people around you. Call, write or visit someone you know who might be lonely, read to someone who can't, offer to help a neighbor, befriend a new friend, learn how to save a life, offer to baby-sit for someone who needs you, shovel snow or rake leaves for someone who can't, help collect food for a food bank or volunteer wherever you are needed. Brainstorm and compile or consult a list of area groups, organizations and individuals that could use your help.

Getting Better All the Time

Have you ever wanted to improve yourself in some way? There's no better time than the new year to make a change. Resolve to get fit, take better care of your teeth, be more cheerful, become a better reader, be nicer to your friends, help out at home more, do better in school, eat more healthy food or become a better bike rider.

Get Something Started: Launch a 2000 Club

Start a 2000 Club with the criteria for becoming a member having something to do with 2000–what else? Exclusive membership can be available to those who can correctly spell 2000 words; answer 2000 math facts; write a 2000-word story; run, skate, hike or bike 2000 meters; do 2000 good deeds or have 2000 great ideas for the future. What is your 2000 Club going to do to make the year 2000 a great one? Make a list of 2000 things your members want to do this year.

Resolve to Make the World a Better Place

Discussion

Do you think changing one event in time would have much impact on the future?

What changes do you hope to see in the future?

What can you do to make the future a better place?

What are you doing to help the environment?

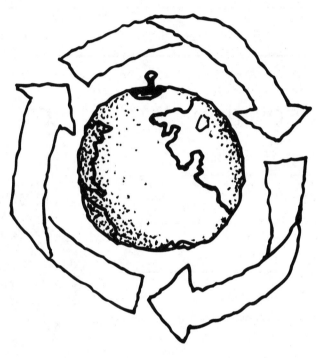

Go Green!

One of the best ways that you can help to make the world a better place is by going green for the new millennium. Caring for the Earth is a very important task and you *can* make a difference to the air we breathe, the water we drink and the habitats we live in. Just like charity, caring for the environment starts at home. Here some ideas to get you started!

Make some resolutions for the environment. Resolve to help the environment in any way you can. Turn to community and worldwide organizations for some guidance, and once you have determined specific areas to focus your energy–resolve to do your best! Your time and talents could instigate or assist a community clean-up, a tree planting blitz, a pollution awareness campaign, recycling rodeo, letter writing and political awareness campaign.

Simple Steps to a Healthier Planet

1. Think about the Earth before you act.

2. Do not support the use of excess packaging. Use reusable containers when you can, do not buy items with too much packaging and let companies know why they have lost your business.

3. Recycle every chance you get.

4. Reuse, share, exchange, trade and pass items on when possible.

5. Walk or bike when you can.

6. Don't litter and clean up trash when it crosses your path.

7. Plant a tree, plant a garden and help to keep the world green.

Challenge

Start an Environment Protection Club in your area.

Raise funds for a worthy organization that helps to keep our planet healthy.

In 1985 a British survey discovered a hole in the ozone layer. By 1989 80 nations had signed an agreement to limit the use of chlorofluorocarbons (CFCs) to protect the ozone layer.

Look at Me in the Year 2000!

Draw a picture of yourself in the year 2000.

I am good at _____

I am pretty good at _____

I hope to get better at _____

This year I hope to _____

_____

My New Year's Resolution

In the new year I resolve to _____

_____

_____

_____

Signed _____

My Anti-Resolutions for the New Year

In the new year I will try not to:

1. _____

2. _____

3. _____

4. _____

Make a Fortune-Teller: Find Out the Future!

You can foretell the future with a fortune-teller of sorts. It has been used by kids for years for fun and predictions.

Materials

1 square piece of paper

pencil, pen, markers or crayons

What to Do

1. Fold the paper diagonally in half both ways and mark the center point with a dot.

2. Fold the corners in towards the center so the points meet at the center dot.

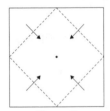

Step 2

Step 2

3. Flip the small square over and fold the corners to the center once again.

4. Fold this square in half one way, open it and then do so the other way.

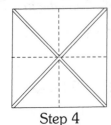

Step 4

5. Gently pull the center point down and push your thumb and forefingers into the four pockets on the sides.

Step 5

Step 5

6. Remove your fingers and turn the square over. Print one word on each corner square. These four words might be colors, sports, flowers, music groups, bugs or any other group of words that offer children choice.

Step 6

7. Flip the square over again and print one numeral on each small triangle. Smaller numbers make the game go faster.

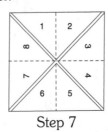

Step 7

8. Fold the triangles out and print a fortune on each folded half. These fortunes might contain trivia or nonsense.

Step 8

9. Fold the fortune corners back down to hide the secrets within.

10. Place fingers and thumbs back into the paper pockets, and prepare to tell fortunes!

11. First ask participants to select one of the four visible selections. When they do, spell the word they chose, flipping the pockets in and out as you do so.

12. After the spelling, the participant chooses one of the numbers that is visible. Flip fingers back and forth again, and stop when the counting is complete.

13. At this point the participant selects one of the numbers and the fortune provided for that number is read.

The Charades of Time

What's a party without a little fun and games? Liven up your celebration with this game of guess the timely phrase.

Materials

timer

paper slips

hat or container

Get Started

Print time-honored sayings on slips of paper. These can be submitted by students or prepared ahead of time by the teacher or game leader.

Place the slips into a hat.

Divide the group into at least two teams of two to six players.

Here are some time-honored expressions to get you started.

A stitch in time saves nine.

The sands of time.

Time waits for no man.

There's no time like the present.

A race against time.

Time heals all wounds.

There's never enough time.

Time is a'wasting.

How to Play

1. Set the timer for one to three minutes.

2. The first team chooses a player to pick a slip of paper and act out the item without speaking. The player's team attempts to guess the item. If the team guesses the item in the allotted time, they get a point. If the time runs out, they do not. In either case, play passes to the next team.

3. The next team picks a slip and plays the game in the same way and so on until every player has had the opportunity to act out an item.

Charade Lingo

Introduce players to the various actions used in a game of charades.

To indicate:

we're starting	*spread palms, facedown*
number of words in a phrase	*hold up one finger for each word*
whole item will be conveyed at once	*draw a large encompassing circle in the air*
miming each word separately	*hold up the number of fingers to show the position of the word in the item*
constituent syllables	*hold up fingers to indicate the number of syllables and tap them on the forearm*
particular syllable	*tap the number of fingers to show the position of the syllable in the word*
a/an	*rounding the index finger and thumb*
the	*T shape using the index fingers*
sounds like	*pull on ear*

New Year's Prediction Cookies

Whip up a batch of fortunes for the new year!

Materials

large bowl

mixer

measuring cup

egg lifter

measuring spoons (tablespoon)

4 egg whites

1/2 (120 ml) cup rice flour

3/4 (180 ml) cup sugar

pinch of salt

1/2 (120 ml) cup melted margarine

2 T. (30 ml) water

cookie tray

What to Do

1. Preheat oven to 350°F (190°C) and grease the cookie tray.

2. Separate the egg whites from the yolks.

3. Put the whites in the large mixing bowl (save the yolks for later).

4. Beat the egg whites until they are frothy and stand in little peaks.

5. Add the dry ingredients and beat for two minutes.

6. Add margarine and water and blend until the mixture looks like thick cream.

7. Drop about 2 tablespoons (30 ml) of mix onto a well-greased cookie tray.

8. Cook for 8 minutes or until the edges are brown. Remove from the oven.

9. Remove one cookie from the tray with an egg lifter.

10. Remove one cookie at a time, leaving the others to stay warm and moldable on the tray. Put your New Year's messages and fortunes inside the cookie and then shape the cookie closed. The cookies will need to be warm to work with, but don't shape them when they are too hot.

Swamp Cheers

Make your own concoction to toast the new year. Consider combinations of ice and ginger ale, cranberry juice, lemonade, orange juice, frozen maraschino cherries or strawberries and lemon or lime slices.

Fresh Baked New Year's Loaf

Fill the air with the ancient aroma of freshly baked bread and turn an art into a festive feast! Shape your dough into the numbers 2000 for added effect.

Bibliography

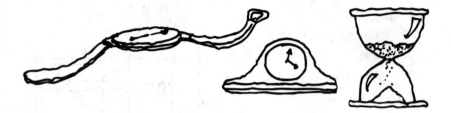

Arnold, Guy. *Datelines of World History*. Warwick Press/ Kingfisher, New York, 1983.

Boslough, John. "Enigma of Time," *National Geographic*, March 1990, pp. 109-132.

Caselli, Giovanni. *Life Through the Ages*. Dorling Kindersley, Inc., New York, 1992.

Clements, Gillian. *The Picture History of Great Inventors*. Alfred A. Knopf, New York, 1994.

Eagan, Robynne. Illustrations by Gary Hoover. *Indoor Games That Teach: Activities for Learning and Fun*. Teaching & Learning Company, Illinois, 1996.

Evans-Pritchard, Professor Sir Edward, Supervisory Editor of the Series, *Peoples of the Earth*; volume twenty: *The Future of Mankind*; Supervisory Editor of the Series; Robert B. Clarke, The Danbury Press, a division of Grolier Enterprises Inc., 1973, Europa Verlag, Italy.

Gega, Peter C. *Science in Elementary Education*, 6th edition, Macmillan Publishing Company, New York, 1990.

Kahn, Herman, and Anthony J. Wiener. *The Year 2000: A Framework for Speculation on the Next Thirty-Three Years*, The Macmillan Company, New York, Collier-Macmillan Canada Ltd., 1967.

Kramer, Ann (senior editor). *The Random House Children's Encyclopedia*. Dorling Kindersley Limited, London, England, 1991.

Magdalen Bear, and Lou Pamenter. *Canadian Days: A Calendar for All Time*. Pembroke Publishers Limited, Ontario, 1990.

Neal, Harry Edward, *The Mystery of Time*. Julian Messner, New York, 1966.

Norris, Doreen, and Joyce Boucher. *Observing Children in the Formative Years*. The Board of Education for the City of Toronto, Toronto, 1989.

Parry, Caroline. *Let's Celebrate! Canada's Special Days*. Kids Can Press Ltd., Toronto, 1987.

Ricker, John, and John Saywell. *The Story of Western Man Series: Greece, The Greatness of Man*. Clarke, Irwin & Company Limited, Toronto/Vancouver, 1973.

Science Framework for California Public Schools, Kindergarten Through Grade Twelve, Adopted by the California State Board of Education, California Department of Education, Sacramento, 1990.

Siegel, Alice, and Maro McLoone Basta. *The Information Please Kids' Almanac*. Houghton Mifflin Company. Boston/New York/London, 1992.

Stein, Sara. Photographs by Rona Beame. *The Evolution Book*. Workman Publishing, New York, 1986.

The Guinness Book of Records, Bantam Books, New York, 1996.

"Toys Were Us," *Time Machine, the American History Magazine for Kids*. December 1996/January 1997 issue, in partnership with the National Museum of American History/Smithsonian Institution.

Turvey, Peter. Created and designed by David Salariya. *Time Lines Inventions: Inventors and Ingenious Ideas*. Franklin Watts, 1992, New York/London/Toronto/Sydney.